The Landscape of Pastoral Learning

A handbook of goals and objectives
with bilingual references for Pastoral Learning
in the parish setting.

Ronald R. Rojas

authorHOUSE®

AuthorHouse™
1663 Liberty Drive
Bloomington, IN 47403
www.authorhouse.com
Phone: 833-262-8899

Published by AuthorHouse 07/29/2021

ISBN: 978-1-6655-3307-2 (sc)
ISBN: 978-1-6655-3306-5 (e)

Library of Congress Control Number: 2021915301

Print information available on the last page.

Any people depicted in stock imagery provided by Getty Images are models, and such images are being used for illustrative purposes only. Certain stock imagery © Getty Images.

NIHIL OBSTAT-06/7/2021
Very Rev. Joseph L. Waters
Censor Librorum

MPRIMATUR-06/07/2021
Most Rev. Gregory L. Parkes
Bishop of St. Petersburg

This book is printed on acid-free paper.

CONTENTS

INTRODUCTION AND PURPOSE

This handbook is intended to provide a comprehensive view of pastoral learning goals and objectives that serve various pastoral formation needs. Since the 2012 publication of the book *The Challenges of Pastoral Leadership: Concepts and Practice* (ISBN 978-1-4772-5632-9), I have dedicated a large portion of my diaconate ministry to the pastoral dimension of formation and have gathered many recommendations, insights, and practices from clergy and lay leaders from over 60 parishes in the United States and Puerto Rico.

This effort's motivation originated from Dan Gast's invitation to participate as parish consultant for *Project Inspire*, Archdiocese of Chicago (2002-2013). Further inspiration was provided by the experiences of being a parish business manager in two different parishes. Other experiences of advising, coaching, or mentoring over twenty fine pastors-administrators. More importantly, serving as a parish administrator for Our Lady of Guadalupe in the diocese of St Petersburg (Florida) for 14 months until a priest could be assigned provided a "hands-on" perspective of the leadership challenges and further motivated pastoral learning interest. These experiences' overall effect added valuable insights for *The Challenges of Pastoral Leadership: Concepts and Practice*.

After the publication of *The Challenges of Pastoral Leadership: Concepts and Practice* came workshops, days of reflection, and courses on pastoral learning topics for the laity, diaconate formation, and seminarians. Much of the book's content has been used in diocesan lay formation programs, such as the Lay Pastoral Ministry Institute (LPMI) from the Diocese of St. Petersburg, Florida, and the Diaconate Formation Program for the same diocese. To some extent, the book was also used in other diocese and seminaries.

There are two guiding principles that provide context and motivation for this handbook. First and foremost is the definition of *formation*, which goes beyond the effects of secular education at the college level or training for an occupation. Formation—as understood by the Church— is centered on cooperation with God's grace:

Formation, as the Church understands it, is not equivalent to a secular sense of schooling or, even less, job training. Formation is first and foremost cooperation with the grace of God." (PPF5, n.68).

This definition provides context for the handbook. The second guiding principle provides its motivation, which is that of being able to provide a landscape of clearly articulated goals and objectives that both the seminarian and the parish can use to assess pastoral learning:

> The goals and objectives of the pastoral formation program should be clearly stated and serve as the basis for the evaluation of seminarians in this area. This statement should also include a description of professional ministerial ethics. (PPF, n.244)

To assume that cooperation with the grace of God occurs exclusively within the confines of the seminary boundaries is shortsighted. Indeed, the parish setting with its variety of learning opportunities contributes to the formation of seminarians as long as their efforts are also aligned with God's cooperating grace. Therefore, the benefits of other forms of learning in the parish, such as mentoring, coaching, personal interactions, and group experiential processing, can only enhance the learning endeavors as long as they also follow the Church's guidance. In fact, participation of parish collaborators within this context can be considered an expectation of priestly formation:

> In addition to onsite supervisors, others collaborating in the various ministries, as well as those served, should be asked to participate in the evaluation of seminarians in ministry (PPF, n250).

But capturing the voice of the Spirt and collaborating with seminary formation in the parish requires specific actions that go beyond just strengthening discernment skills and delineating pastoral goals and objectives. It requires an active spiritual awareness, a keen receptivity to God's grace, and an effective learning environment. These requirements provide the rationale for suggesting the concept of Teaching Parish, a model that parallels the Teaching Hospital.

Further maturation and bi-cultural validation of these concepts were conducted over six years of offering a parish administration course to seminarians of the St. Vincent de Paul Regional Seminary in Boynton Beach, Florida. Here I owe a debt of gratitude to the seminarians, staff, and rectors of this regional, bilingual seminary. More specifically, my gratitude goes to the past Rector and now Bishop of Diocese of Beaumont, Texas, Most Rev. David Toups, and the current Rector, Very Rev. Alfredo Hernandez. In his book *Formation activities & Catholic Seminarians: A practical Theological study of their impact on Subsequent perseverance in ministry,* Very Rev. Hernandez highlights the value of the pastoral experience to maturation permanence of the vocation. Furthermore, being able to assist the Chicago seminary at Mundelein (University of St. Mary of the Lake) with assessments and proposals for improving the Tolton Teaching Parish Program provided additional insights into the teaching-learning dynamics in the parish setting, given their efforts to form seminarians within a range of over 75 parishes. In this case, I am grateful to Fr. Maina Waithaka, then Dean of Formation, and to its Rector, Very Rev. John Kartje. Also, I owe a debt of gratitude to the reviewers of this manuscript: Sister Nadiya Levchenko, Paul Hilliard, Sister Mary Aloysius Onwuegbuchulam, Very Rev. Joseph Waters, and Father John Lipscomb. Their insights, observations, and suggestions helped enhance the practical value of this handbook.

The language and structure of this handbook are for primary use in English, although the objectives and goals are referenced in Spanish, as indicated in the subtitle. Two factors influence this approach. First, the handbook is heavily rooted in its origins, namely, the seminarians at St Vincent de Paul in Boynton Beach (a bilingual seminary) and those at the University of St. Mary of the Lake (USML) Mundelein. At least for now, my exposure to them shows that English is the primary learning language and supplemented with references in Spanish. That explains why there is more English than Spanish, especially at the beginning (Instructions) and at the end (syllabus). A second factor is the potential use of the handbook at the parish, which is a resource for the Vocation Mentoring Board (team, committee). So far, a significant number of these mentoring boards (or teams, committees) deal primarily in English, with just a few Spanish parishes. A similar argument is made for the men in the permanent

INSTRUCTIONS FOR THIS RESOURCE

The purpose of this handbook is to serve as a reference in providing a comprehensive list of objectives and goals related to pastoral learning in parish life. Those experienced in pastoral formation realize that *pastoral experiences* are best converted into *pastoral learning* when adequately targeted, practiced, and processed. Having a broader view of possible goals and objectives allows formators and mentors to suggest actions that are better articulated and tailored to the pastoral growth needs of those undergoing pastoral formation.

Truthfully, the primary focus of this handbook is on seminarian pastoral formation in the parish setting. Yet much of what is said applies to the pastoral formation of permanent deacons and laity. For seminarians, this resource is a wide window into selecting the most appropriate objectives and goals needed to nurture and appropriate the priestly vocation. Seminarian formators benefit from this resource by having a greater selection of learning objectives and goals than just a simple template of parish activities. The formation programs for permanent deacons can benefit from this resource since its landscape of parish activities can help identify gaps in parish experiences that may be relevant to the vocation discernment process. This handbook is also applicable to lay leaders and the recently instituted ministry of catechists (*Antiquum ministerium*, May 11, 2021) as they grow in appreciating pastoral sensitivities that may be absent from their current ministry endeavors.

To be clear, the reference to "secular models" used throughout this handbook refers to commercialized training programs offered by many businesses and corporations to their managers and supervisors, as well as models available in the academic disciplines of management and leadership. The concern is that these "business-academic" models were built for a specific context—and although many models may have some value to the parish setting—they tend to exclude significant expectations such as Divine Providence, discernment, prayer, and nurturing a sense of communion. Still, engaging in administration, management, and leadership processes is a task for everyone, including the priesthood (CCL,1284).

There are two guiding principles that provide context and motivation for this handbook. First and foremost is the definition of *formation*, which goes beyond the effects of secular education at the college level or training for an occupation. Formation—as understood by the Church— is centered on cooperation with God's grace:

> Formation, as the Church understands it, is not equivalent to a secular sense of schooling or, even less, job training. Formation is first and foremost cooperation with the grace of God." (PPF5, n.68).

This definition provides context for the handbook and provides a critical criterion for the efforts in this handbook on pastoral learning. It affords the parish with guidance that connects with the seminary's endeavors across all dimensions, introduces the necessity of discernment processes, and alerts the parish to go beyond just "job training" for the seminarians. In fact, the Program of Priestly Formation (5th edition) states,

> The pastoral formation program should provide seminarians with a broad exposure to supervised pastoral service, with primary emphasis on parish ministry" (n.246).

Along with this guidance, there is also the need to recognize the distinction between the ministerial priesthood and the priesthood of all believers. As a reference, this distinction is stated in the *Instruction on Certain Questions Regarding the Collaboration of the Non-ordained Faithful in the Sacred Ministry of Priest (Libreria Editrice Vaticana, Vatican City 15 August 1997, the Solemnity of the Assumption of the Blessed Virgin Mary)*.

The second guiding principle provides its motivation, which is that of being able to provide a landscape of clearly articulated goals and objectives that both the seminarian and the parish can use to assess pastoral learning:

> The goals and objectives of the pastoral formation program should be clearly stated and serve as the basis for the evaluation of seminarians in this area. This statement should also include a description of professional ministerial ethics. (PPF, n.244)

In following the definition of "formation" expressed above, to assume that cooperation with the grace of God from for the pastoral dimension occurs exclusively within the confines of the seminary boundaries is shortsighted. Within the aim and settings for pastoral formation, the parish has a significant role (PPF5, n. 239). Indeed, the parish setting with its variety of learning opportunities contributes to the formation of seminarians as long as their efforts are also aligned with God's cooperating grace. Therefore, the benefits of other forms of learning available in the parish, such as mentoring, coaching, personal interactions, and group experiential processing, can only enhance the pastoral learning endeavors provided they also follow the Church's guidance. In fact, participation of parish collaborators within this context can be considered an expectation of priestly formation:

> In addition to onsite supervisors, others collaborating in the various ministries, as well as those served, should be asked to participate in the evaluation of seminarians in ministry (PPF, n250).

But capturing the voice of the Spirt and collaborating with seminary formation in the parish requires specific actions that go beyond just strengthening discernment skills and delineating pastoral goals and objectives. It requires an active spiritual awareness, a keen receptivity to God's grace, and an effective learning environment. These requirements provide the rationale for suggesting the concept of Teaching Parish, a model that parallels the Teaching Hospital.

For the most part, opportunities for pastoral experiences in the parish setting seem to be working satisfactorily. Seminaries, diaconate formation programs, and lay leadership development activities continue benefitting from pastors and parishes willing to contribute to pastoral skills' growth and development. But what can be done to further refine pastoral formation programs in the parish setting?

For institutions, pastors, and parish mentors, this handbook suggests five conceptual underpinnings to improve the mindset that drives the pastoral learning environment in a parish setting and defines a Teaching Parish: (a) the significance of the term "vocation," (b) Church guidance for pastoral learning, (c) principles of experiential learning, (d) the difference between career mentoring and pastoral mentoring, and (e) the value of group processing of pastoral experiences.

A brief background and rationale for each conceptual underpinning of each of the five conceptual areas of improvement are described next.

Understanding "vocation"

Understanding the meaning of "vocation" and "calling" is foundational to pastoral learning. The most popular interpretation of "vocation"—at least from a purely secular view—is the presumption that it reflects a specific occupation, job, or profession. Here the risk to pastoral learning is that parish experiences become constrained to performing optimally to a ministry "job description." For example, one can easily recall cases where either a Eucharistic Minister, Lector, Sacristan, or parish administrative employee have portrayed their ministries as "jobs" more than pastoral learning opportunities for themselves. The assigned services are rendered, but it seems the mechanics of the tasks are more relevant than the prospects of translating these experiences into forms of learning that foster their vocation. Unknowingly, they may emulate too many behaviors learned in their secular jobs or occupations in parish life. In very few cases have they been mentored into an understanding of how these ministry experiences impact their own vocation (calling) development. They have yet to see that ministry assignments are much more than just performing against a job description.

To be sure, the secular workplace occupies a central part of secular life, where favorable and adverse situations can contribute to the "shaping the story" of one's calling and identity. Still, at a deeper level, vocation implies a lot more. As an example of this limited interpretation, we talk about a vocation for medicine, education, engineering, science, and so on. It's not wrong to relate the term vocation to a career, but this notion only partially resonates with a deeper reality.

It is understandable that the word "vocation" and "call" tend to be used interchangeably in the secular world, as the word vocation derives from the Latin word "vocare" that translates to call. But the vocation is more than just an orientation toward religious consecration or a "call" for a form of employment or occupation.

In its most authentic form, a vocation (calling) emerges from the unique and unrepeatable truth of what it is to be a person, from the "self" as envisioned by God even before one existed in the flesh. It is the "original idea" of every person already thought by God from all eternity:

> If our human statistics, human categories, human political, economic, and social systems, and mere human possibilities fail to ensure that man can be born, live, and act as one who is unique and unrepeatable, then all this is ensured by God. For God and before God, the human being is always unique and unrepeatable, somebody thought of and chosen from eternity, some called and identified by his own name. (St. John Paul II, Urbi et Orbi, Christmas 1978).

The vocation (calling) of each person is rooted and revealed by one's "name" (one could call it one's "ontological name" as opposed to the given name by one's parents), the "whole" self as created by God:

> When God calls a person by name, he reveals at the same time his vocation, his plan of holiness and good, by which that person will become someone unique and a gift to others. (Pope Francis, Message of the Pope for XXXIII World Youth Day).

The revelation of the vocation (calling) occurs within this "being called by name" and slowly becomes evident by the examining and interpreting of day-to-day experiences:

> In fact, from eternity God has thought of us and has loved us as unique individuals. Every one of us he called by name, as the Good Shepherd "calls his sheep by name" (Jn 10:3). However, only in the unfolding of the history of our lives and its events is the eternal plan of God revealed to each of us. Therefore, it is a gradual process; in a certain sense, one that happens day by day. (Christifidelis laici, n. 58)

In particular, those parishioners associated more closely with seminarian formation must be aware that the priestly vocation and identity is also one that needs to be appropriated, which is much more than being pastorally experienced, articulate in prayer, solemn in liturgies, spiritually strong, and knowledgeable of scripture and doctrine:

> In virtue of the grace of Holy Orders, a priest is able to stand and act in the community in the name and person of Jesus Christ, Head and Shepherd of the Church. This sacramental character needs to be completed by the personal and pastoral formation of the priest, who appropriates "the mind of Christ" and effectively communicates the mysteries of faith through his human personality as a bridge, through his personal witness of faith rooted in his spiritual life, and through his knowledge of faith. These elements of formation converge in pastoral formation (PPF, n. 237).

In particular, those parishioners associated more closely with seminarian formation must be aware that the priestly vocation and identity is also one that needs to be appropriated, which is much more than being pastorally experienced, articulate in prayer, solemn in liturgies, spiritually strong, and knowledgeable of scripture and doctrine:

> In virtue of the grace of Holy Orders, a priest is able to stand and act in the community in the name and person of Jesus Christ, Head and Shepherd of the Church. This sacramental character needs to be completed by the personal and pastoral formation of the priest, who appropriates "the mind of Christ" and effectively communicates the mysteries of faith through his human personality as a bridge, through his personal witness of faith rooted in his spiritual life, and through his knowledge of faith. These elements of formation converge in pastoral formation (PPF, n. 237).

Specifically, the framework of pastoral learning for seminarians is presented in the USCCB's Program for Priestly Formation (PPF), Section IV of the fifth edition, and "The Gift of the Priestly Vocation" (*Ratio Fundamentalis Institutionis Sacerdotalis*). These documents are readily available, so, therefore, it is unnecessary to replicate or summarize them here. Yet it is valuable to highlight n.236 of the PPF (5th Edition) where the value of pastoral learning is deemed as the culmination of the entire formation process:

All four pillars of formation are interwoven and go forward concurrently. Still, in a certain sense, pastoral formation is the culmination of the entire formation process: "The whole formation imparted to candidates for the priesthood aims at preparing them to enter into communion with the charity of Christ the Good Shepherd. Hence, their formation in its different aspects must have a fundamentally pastoral character" (Pastores dabo vobis, no. 57).

The first conceptual underpinning suggested as improvements to the mindset of pastoral learning in the parish setting is recognizing that pastoral experiences are more than just an appraisal of performance against a series of tasks. A clear relationship between ministry objectives and their intent in promoting discovery and fulfillment of the vocation starts with a clear understanding of vocation as a calling. Ministry tasks provide opportunities to facilitate the unfolding of a vocation (calling) rooted in the "original idea" of every person already thought by God from all eternity. Having a better appreciation of "vocation," providing experiences, and facilitating the interpretation and learning of those experiences is at the heart of vocational search.

Church guidance for pastoral learning

Having an appreciation of the Church's desire to recognize pastoral learning intends to ensure that the outcomes are aligned with formation objectives. Understanding the theological and practical expectations of the Church is paramount in safeguarding the context of pastoral learning and its relationship with other aspects of formation, namely, the spiritual, human, and intellectual dimensions of formation. Accordingly, the Church provides specific guidance regarding the pastoral formation of clergy and the laity.

Specifically, the framework of pastoral learning for seminarians is presented in the USCCB's Program for Priestly Formation (PPF), Section IV of the fifth edition. The document is readily available, so, therefore, it is unnecessary to replicate or summarize here. Yet it is valuable to highlight n.236 of the PPF (5th Edition) where the value of pastoral learning is deemed as the culmination of the entire formation process:

All four pillars of formation are interwoven and go forward concurrently. Still, in a certain sense, pastoral formation is the culmination of the entire formation process: "The whole formation imparted to candidates for the priesthood aims at preparing them to enter into communion with the charity of Christ the Good Shepherd. Hence, their formation in its different aspects must have a fundamentally pastoral character" (Pastores dabo vobis, no. 57).

The pastoral objectives listed in this handbook have "tags" to highlight their relationship with the other formation dimensions. For example, the fifth objective in the first section of the handbook says:

5. Recognize the importance of following the pastoral learning agreement (H, S, I, P).

The letters in parentheses for this objective (H, S, I, P) indicate this objective relates to the Human, Spiritual, Intellectual, and Pastoral dimensions. All other objectives are "tagged" based upon their connections with the dimensions of formation.

Two distinct forms of pastoral experiences in the parish setting are evident within seminary formation. One form is intended to provide foundational experiences of parish life related to the vocation discovery. The second form is more intense and oriented towards the administrative and leadership expectations within the priestly vocation. One form is intended to provide a broad exposure to parish life, and the other is focused on learning leadership responsibilities. Table 1 offers a more detailed explanation of the differences between these two forms.

Just as academia recognizes that Management and Leadership are two separate but interrelated disciplines, Parish Administration and Pastoral Leadership are treated in the same way. Notably, many of the administrative and leadership expectations from the priestly vocation are outlined in "The priest, pastor and leader of the parish community", an instruction issued by the Congregation for the Clergy, August 4, 2002. This instruction is fundamental to correctly align the parish leadership formation for seminarians and priests. Naturally, it is also essential to keep track of all revision updates and relevant supporting sources addressing seminarian formation's pastoral dimension.

Table 1. Comparing Pastoral Programs

	Pastoral Learning Fundamentals	Pastoral Leadership Learning
Priorities	Engage in **parish life experiences** that help the seminarian apply the dimensions of formation.	Engage in **parish leadership experiences** that help the seminarian understand parish operations from a parochial administrator-pastor view.
Ecclesial Guidance	Program for Priestly Formation (PPF), latest edition, Section IV, Pastoral Formation.	*The Priest, Pastor, and Leader of the Parish Community* (4 August 2002). Offices of the Congregation for the Clergy: Rome.
Focus	Ensure parish life experiences through community mentoring.	Ensure processing of operational experiences through community mentoring.
Pre-requisites	Willingness to recognize and select areas of personal growth.	Willingness to understand and engage in leadership roles of parish life.
Expectations	The seminarian will engage in a variety of interpersonal, liturgical, and ministry group experiences.	The seminarian will engage in the fundamentals of parish management and leadership processes.
Outcomes	Exposure to experiences that enrich his pastoral sensitivity and help in the maturation of his vocation.	Familiarization and experiences with parochial administrator/pastor functions.

A similar document describes the Church's expectations for the pastoral formation of permanent deacons. *The National Directory for the formation, ministry, and life of Permanent Deacons in the United States* recognizes again the human, spiritual, intellectual, and pastoral dimensions of formation. It describes specific pastoral expectations for the aspirant and candidate in chapters 5 and 6, and therefore, should be considered as further guidance to the diaconate objectives and goals presented in this handbook. Although again it is unnecessary to repeat here what is stated in this document, it is worth studying both the PPF and *The National Directory for the Formation, Ministry, and Life of Permanent Deacons* to recognize their similarities and differences.

Finally, guidance for the pastoral formation of the laity can be found in the Post-synodal Apostolic Exhortation, *Christifidelis laici*. The document addresses the reciprocal efforts between clergy and laity concerning pastoral learning:

> Priests and religious ought to assist the lay faithful in their formation. In this regard the Synod Fathers have invited priests and candidates for Orders to "be prepared carefully so that they are ready to foster the vocation and mission of the lay faithful"[219]. In turn, the lay faithful themselves can and should help priests and religious in the course of their spiritual and pastoral journey (n.61).

Pastoral emphasis for the recently instituted ministry of catechist can be found in Pope Francis' apostolic letter issued motu proprio, *Antiquum ministerium:*

> They should also receive suitable biblical, theological, pastoral, and pedagogical formation to be competent communicators of the truth of the faith and they should have some prior experience of catechesis (cf. SECOND VATICAN ECUMENICAL COUNCIL, Decree on the Pastoral Office of Bishops in the Church *Christus Dominus*, 14; CIC can. 231 §1; CCEO can. 409 §1). (n.8)

Hence, the second conceptual underpinning suggested as improvements to pastoral learning mindset in the parish setting is familiarization with Church guidance. A study of these documents is essential to ensure proper alignment with Church intent.

Principles of Experiential Learning

Having pastoral experiences is just the first of a two-step process. Experiences alone miss the purpose of pastoral formation. Experiences are formative when they are converted into learning. Here is where a few experiential learning fundamentals as a conceptual underpinning can further refine pastoral formation programs.

Experiential learning is an activity that translates academic theory into practice. Specifically, experiential learning is a process that involves students in activities that are considered "academically meaningful" where theoretical concepts intersect with praxis and personal development. A key to engage learners is to incorporate active learning strategies into the curriculum (Delialioglu, 2011; Goldberg & Ingram, 2011, Hayden, et al. 2011). Active learning strategies refer to effective ways to engage in activities based on how people learn (Walker, 2003). In the case of seminarians, this points to why pastoral learning is considered an integral part of the seminary curriculum.

But experiential learning is also self-directed. In its broadest meaning, self-directed learning describes a process in which learners take the initiative, with or without the help of others, in diagnosing their learning needs, formulating learning goals, identifying human and material resources for learning, choosing, and implementing appropriate learning (Jiusto & DiBiasio, 2006).

As a third conceptual underpinning to improve the mindset that drives the pastoral learning environment in a parish setting, there is an opportunity to assess the effectiveness of experiential learning principles, specifically the parish efforts to sustain academic relevance, personal development, and self-directed learning. To what degree does the pastoral setting help put theoretical knowledge into practice? How well do the parish experiences foster personal discernment and development for the learner's vocation? If experiential learning is a function of the level of personal involvement, then to what extent is the learning climate in the parish truly engaging the learner?

Again, experiences are formative when they are converted into learning, and of the four dimensions, pastoral formation is the dimension that is mostly self-directed. The intellectual, spiritual, and human dimensions of formation are more structured in their learning approaches. But the effectiveness of the pastoral dimension relies more on the initiatives of the learner. The improvement opportunities offered by this third conceptual underpinning stem from recognizing and stimulating pastoral learning as a learner-centered activity.

Cultivating Pastoral Mentoring Skills

A fourth conceptual underpinning suggested as an improvement to the mindset of pastoral learning in the parish setting is to cultivate pastoral mentoring. This form of mentoring is unique to the Church setting because it is closely associated with the concept of formation. Having professional "formators" in the parish would require in itself a more comprehensive understanding of the demeanors and techniques more commonly used in the seminary. Yet "pastoral mentoring" seems a better fit because it is related to formation, and to a large extent, is already occurring in parish life.

However, there are two commonly used teaching models observed in parish life from the secular sector that, although valuable, may require clarification when applied to pastoral learning. The two teaching models are "coaching" and "business mentoring." These teaching models are prevalent in parish life because they represent the two most pervasive metaphors used in our western culture: sports and business (Liu, 2002). Coaching is a derivative of the sports metaphor, and mentoring emerges as a teaching model from the business metaphor.

To coach is to improve task performance. A triathlon coach monitors and analyzes all aspects of conditioning and competition, whether it be swimming, biking, running, racing, nutrition, strength training, exercise science, kinematics, or equipment. The coach's focus is on enhancing performance. Coaching for performance in the pastoral setting occurs when performance expectations are less than optimal. An example is when a seminarian teaching a CCD class needs coaching to become a better instructor. The observations and insights offered to the seminarian are limited to improving performance within a narrow context.

The coaching model of teaching for improved performance is a component of learning but limited in focus, relationship, and horizon, whereas the mentoring model has broader implications. A complete distinction between coaching and mentoring is presented in Table 2:

Table 2. Comparing Coaching and Mentoring

Attribute	Coaching	Mentoring
Objective	Improve performance	Guide personal development
Focus	Tasks at hand	Talents and abilities
Initiative	Coach directed	Self-directed
Duration	Short term implications	Long term implications
Feedback	Corrective actions	Insights
Relationship	Must agree with coach	Must discern choices
Horizon	Specialty driven	Total person

Mentoring is considered a better teaching model for the pastoral setting because it supports many experiential learning principles. While mentoring addresses a more comprehensive set of developmental opportunities, it also supports self-directed principles. But still, business mentoring is focused on improving career opportunities (Ragins, 2012), whereas ministry is more than just a career.

To speak of "career mentoring" for a seminarian, a priest, or a deacon is to miss the point about vocation development. This is the main difference between "workplace mentoring" and "pastoral mentoring." All mentoring is conducted within a specific context, and the parish setting is the context for pastoral mentoring. Therefore, pastoral mentoring is a unique teaching model where experiences are shared as insights into vocational discovery and maturation. A fuller comparison of business mentoring and pastoral mentoring is presented in Table 3.

Table 3. Comparing workplace and pastoral mentoring

Workplace Mentoring	Pastoral Mentoring
Progression along career development	Progression along a vocation and calling
Developing career opportunities	Developing the priestly vocation
Trajectory viewed and nurtured from an organizational context	Trajectory viewed and nurtured from a community context
Learning to increase professional value	Learning for vocation discovery and validation
Professional identity is self-constructed, composed by circumstances-opportunities	Vocation is discovered and fulfilled trough discernment processes
Relies on the more evident attributes, talents, energies, and abilities.	Relies on God's calling and personal uniqueness
Heavily task oriented, influenced by occupation or professional aspirations.	Relationally oriented, influenced by God's calling
Identity is an autonomous designed way to secure uniqueness (professional identity)	Identity is an eternally designed uniqueness (vocation as identity)

As a reminder, pastoral mentoring as presented here is not intended only for clergy. There is an opportunity to apply pastoral mentoring as a teaching model throughout the parish, especially in forming ministry leaders and parish staff.

The fourth conceptual underpinning suggested as an improvement to the mindset of pastoral learning in the parish setting is to cultivate pastoral mentoring as the preferred teaching model. Of course, there are prospects within the parish for using coaching and business mentoring, but pastoral mentoring—as defined here— suits the experiential learning principles discussed earlier, is focused on vocational development, and easily encompasses each of the formation dimensions.

Group Processing of Pastoral Experiences

A fifth conceptual underpinning suggested as an improvement to pastoral learning mindset in the parish setting is considering group processing of pastoral experiences.

Indeed, each person engaged in pastoral learning will take time to reflect and process the experiences, therefore converting experiences into learning. Although valuable, this method has some limitations to consider. Here the adage *"You don't know what you don't know"* helps illustrate shortcomings inherent to this method.

There are two ways to demonstrate the value of group processing for pastoral learning. One way is to study what formal research says on the topic, and another way is to understand "blind spots" using the Johari Window model.

A sampling of formal research on the value of group experiences processing highlights the significance of group pastoral learning techniques. Individualized experience processing is inherently subject to blind spots, which would prevent visualizing a fuller impact of experiences if left unattended. Therefore, accepting the existence and effects of blind spots is a first crucial step in recognizing the value of the group processing technique:

> People's beliefs about their personality, or how they typically think, feel, and behave, correspond somewhat to objective accuracy criteria. Yet recent research has highlighted the fact that there are many blind spots in self-knowledge and that these blind spots can have fairly negative consequences (Carlson, 2013).

A most commonly recognized technique to uncover and manage the effects of blind spots on self-knowledge is to involve others, be it one-on-one or in a small group setting. Bollich, Johannet, and Vazire (2011) observe that fuller self-knowledge is best when including others that can offer insights into one's own personality:

> We come to the conclusion that explicit feedback, a largely unexamined path, is likely a fruitful avenue for learning about one's own personality. Specifically, we suggest that self-knowledge might be fully realized through the use of explicit feedback from

close, knowledgeable others. As such, we conclude that the road to self-knowledge likely cannot be traveled alone but must be traveled with close others who can help shed light on our blind spots (Bollich, Johannet, and Vazire, 2011).

This technique of involving others in self-knowledge and experience processing is also an indicator of openness to others. One explanation for the variability of blind spot sizes is the amount and quality of interpersonal comments accepted (e.g., Bollich, Johannet, & Vazire, 2011; Luft & Ingham, 1955; Srivastava, 2012). Less advice from others tends to perpetuate blind spots, and more interaction helps moderate blind spot effects. Consequently, blind spots tend to have sizes that are proportional to relational perceptions:

> Notably, the effect size of the distinctive blind spot varied considerably between targets. Individuals with "larger" blind spots are arguably more "out of touch" with the perceptions that others actually have of them (Gallrein, Weßels, Carlson, & Leising, 2016).

A second way to visualize a broader view of self and issues with blind spots involving others in experiential processing is through the Johari Window, a model developed in 1955 by Joseph Luft and Harry Ingham. This model provides individuals with a broader understanding of themselves and consists of four window "panes" of human interaction: Open Self, Hidden Self, Blind Self, and Unknown Self. The "Open Self" pane denotes actions, behaviors, and information that are known to the learner as well as to those around them. The second quadrant is referred to as the "Blind Self" pane, where actions and behaviors are evident to others but not to the learner. The "Hidden Self" pane represents a view where information is known to the learner but unknown to anyone else. The "Unknown Self" pane refers to information, skills, and behaviors that are unknown to both the learner and others. Combining all these panes provides a more comprehensive view of a learner's capabilities, challenges, blind spots, and perceptual differences. A graphical depiction of these window panes and the relationships with self and others is presented in Table 4.

Table 4. The Johari Window

	Known to self	Unknown to self
Known to others	**OPEN SELF** *Things I know about myself that others also know.*	**BLIND SELF** *Things I don't' know about myself that others know.*
Unknown to others	**HIDDEN SELF** *Things I know about myself that others don't know.*	**UNKNOWN SELF** *Things I don't know about myself that others don't know.*

The Johari Window offers opportunities for validation, discovery, and discernment. Observations from the "Open Self" are readily accepted and validated in conversation with others. The "Hidden Self" provides a source of "healthy self-disclosure" where a learner can give additional insights into experiential processing by offering information previously unknown to others. The "Blind Self" windowpane allows opportunities to uncover learner blind spots. The most challenging pane is the "Unknown Self," where there are undiscovered aspects to both learners and others. This pane suggests discernment, prayer, and openness to God's calling for authentic new findings related to the vocation.

With these two approaches—the formal research and the Johari Window—the value of group processing represents the fifth conceptual improvement to pastoral learning in the parish setting. How these small groups—call them "Vocation Mentoring Boards"— are set up and trained is a function of (a) the criteria agreed upon by the pastor and dean of pastoral formation, (b) the needs of the learner (seminarian), and (c) the composition and training of the small group considering the previous four conceptual improvements (Principles of Experiential Learning, Vocation, Church guidance, and Pastoral Mentoring). Some parishes have temporary groups, whereas other parishes have more permanent vocational teams or pastoral learning committees. This handbook offers a set of criteria for creating Teaching Parishes, a concept that parallels what in the medical education field is called the Teaching Hospital. Regardless, group sharing of pastoral insights enhances the conversion of experiences into learning.

Leadership Models in the Parish Setting

The final topic of discussion is leadership within the pastoral setting. Inevitably, secularly developed leadership models will occupy spheres of influence in the parish setting. This is the fundamental challenge of pastoral leadership. Without a broader understanding of the context, assumptions, and limitations of secular leadership models, many of us will continue to learn and apply (many times awkwardly) the leadership model "de jour" in hopes of becoming better leaders, but to the potential detriment of ministry and parish life.

Most leadership theories have originated primarily from observing social behaviors in the secular world, and until recently, with minimal consideration to spiritual realities. In other words, most of what we know about leadership theories and praxis today was developed based on an incomplete human foundation by observing the interactions of power and influence among individuals and groups but without consideration for the spiritual realities that surround them.

The ability to differentiate between valuable and harmful consequences of secular leadership models in lay pastoral development is the most fundamental challenge of pastoral leadership. Leadership concepts are socially constructed and culturally bound (Mellahi,2000), so applying any secular leadership model to the pastoral sector requires constant and careful examination against the culture and framework of the Catholic Church. Models coming from the business, non-profit, government, military, or academic sectors are built primarily for their respective sectors. Although their availability may lure them into parish life, their indiscriminate use, particularly in sectors for which they were never intended, has already proven to be deeply problematic. Evaluating these models' underlying assumptions and correlating their definitional components to a healthy understanding of the pastoral sector represents a significant first step in acknowledging the unique nature of pastoral leadership. Said differently, a leadership expert or successful practitioner in one sector (secular) will not guarantee success in another sector (parish).

Among the variety of models available within the leadership discipline are those that are competency-based, and for the pastoral setting, there are expected competencies crucial to the exercise of leadership yet lacking in the past and current secular models. Fundamental competencies for the pastoral setting include vocation (calling) awareness, character strength, relational competency, community (which is different from organizational competency), discernment competency (inclusive of prayer, reflection, and contemplation), pastoral awareness (love as a rationale for behavior and action), and a "directing" competency-based upon the orchestration of activities revealed by Divine Providence rather than just by a leader's desires (humility). These same competencies are also valuable criteria in assessing the value and limitations of secular models in the pastoral setting. Again, suffice it to say that while secular models permeate ministry leadership, pastoral leadership as a competency model is the most desirable construct for the parish setting and merits recognition and promulgation. More on this topic is presented in Part 8 of this handbook.

How to Use this Handbook

After establishing a theoretical foundation for a broader conceptual underpinning to improve the pastoral learning mindset in the parish setting, what follows is a basic overview of how to use this handbook as a resource.

Undoubtedly, the broader view of pastoral learning objectives and goals can seem overwhelming. The intent is to provide a more comprehensive set of choices, depending on the learner's developmental needs. It is unrealistic to expect anyone to fulfill every single objective and goal presented here.

In composing a pastoral learning agreement—the planning document typically agreed upon by learner, formator, and pastor defining the desirable learning expectations—targeting one objective or goal from each significant category should suffice to provide direction and accountability. In other words, selecting one objective or goal from the major categories of (a) vocational development, (b) ministry engagement, (c) judgment and decision making, and (d) pastoral awareness would be a minimal expectation. A similar approach is helpful for the diaconate objectives and goals as well as for pastoral leadership development. What matters is an organic, natural growth into critical areas of personal development.

Regarding the relationships and minimal expectations of formators (e.g., seminary), pastor, learner (e.g., seminarian), and group processing opportunities, the recommended method is to establish criteria for a "teaching parish," an approach comparable to what is known as a "teaching hospital." Whereas a teaching hospital is a medical facility affiliated with a medical school where medical students receive practical training, a teaching parish is affiliated with a seminary where seminarians receive practical pastoral formation. The name suggested for this group is the *"Pastoral Learning Board,"* which evokes the advising nature of its purpose. An outline of teaching parish criteria is presented in the later parts of this handbook.

Summary

Converting pastoral experiences into valuable pastoral learning for seminarians, deacons, and the laity is already happening in many parishes. Yet, a deeper view of five conceptual underpinnings is available to help further pastoral learning effectiveness. Precisely, (a) the significance of "vocation," (b) Church guidance, (c) principles of experiential learning, (d) pastoral mentoring, and (e) group processing of pastoral experiences can certainly represent improvements with English and Spanish pastoral learning, more so if a teaching parish approach is adopted.

Hopefully, this handbook will serve its intended purpose while at the same time encouraging further dialogue and research into finding ways to improve pastoral learning in the parish setting.

PART 1 - ESSENTIAL OBJECTIVES AND GOALS

The Landscape of Pastoral Learning

PART 1

Essential Objectives and Goals

This first part of the handbook presents the essential objectives of parish pastoral learning in four sections, namely, objectives related to (a) vocation development, (b) engaging in ministry, (c) judgment and decision making, and (d) pastoral awareness. Each of the objectives within these sections has more specific goals. It's worth noting that most objectives and goals are not directly associated with any particular parish ministry, allowing the learner the flexibility to choose the most appropriate ministry based upon what the assigned parish has to offer. So, for example, Objective 9 *"Recognize the processes needed to conduct effective meetings."* can be applied to Youth Ministry as well as to Prayer Group meetings. Each objective and subsequent goals were designed to allow flexibility in selecting the ministry setting. Of course, it is expected that when composing the Learning Agreement, the specific ministry is also indicated. Notably, the Lector and Acolyte ministries typically require some training before being instituted, and therefore, it was deemed unnecessary to specify goals and objectives in this handbook.

A. Objectives related to Vocation Development

1. Recognize the value of receiving learning insights from others (H, P).

References to the
dimensions of formation:
I = Intellectual
H = Human
S = Spiritual
P = Pastoral

a. Accept insights from interactions with Pastor.

b. Accept insights from peers or mentors in small group sessions.

c. Demonstrate the ability to conduct self-appraisals and identify key learning events based upon learning experiences within the assigned ministries.

2. Recognizes the importance of articulating pastoral experiences within the context of personal growth (H, P).

a. Demonstrate the ability to integrate pastoral learning within the overall context of his formation.
b. Demonstrate the ability to articulate pastoral learning to pastor, formator, and/or mentor group.

3. Recognize the effects of pastoral experiences in the deepening of personal faith maturity (S, P).

a. Demonstrate the ability to seek and fulfill pastoral objectives that are sufficiently challenging towards growing in faith maturity.
b. Demonstrate the ability to develop a mature and humble attitude to an assigned ministry.

4. Recognize the need for taking initiatives within one's capabilities and limitations (H, P).

a. Demonstrate the ability to discern the pastoral needs within at least one of the assigned ministries and offer realistic, value-added solutions.
b. Demonstrate the ability to discern the boundaries where professional assistance or a referral may be required.
c. Demonstrate the ability to effectively apply coping skills when confronted with stresses and strains of parish ministry.

> References to the
> dimensions of formation:
> I = Intellectual
> H = Human
> S = Spiritual
> P = Pastoral

5. Recognize the importance of following the pastoral learning agreement (H, S, I, P).

a. Demonstrate the ability to plan and fulfill the agreed-upon pastoral learning objectives thoughtfully.
b. Demonstrate the ability to recognize workload unbalances and submit recommendations or changes if the objectives are unrealistic (too easy, too difficult).

6. Recognize how personal attitudes, values, and prejudices affect pastoral ministry (H, P).

a. Demonstrate the ability to be available to others while maintaining proper boundaries when engaged in the assigned ministries.
b. Demonstrate the ability to identify and manage personal biases that may limit pastoral effectiveness.
c. Demonstrate the ability to seek opportunities and situations, leading to assess progress in managing biases.

7. Recognize that ministry flows from one's gifts and evolving vocational search (S, P).

References to the dimensions of formation:
I = Intellectual
H = Human
S = Spiritual
P = Pastoral

a. Demonstrate the ability to identify and engage in ministry activities that nurture and challenge personal gifts and vocational pursuits.
b. Demonstrate the ability to recognize and integrate natural creative skills and talents (e.g., art, music, writing, counseling, etc.) into the vocation development.
b. Demonstrate the ability to articulate the effects of pastoral learning and the ongoing development of the vocation.

8. Recognize the developmental value of actively engaging in community dynamics.

a. Demonstrate the ability to experience and share enjoyment with others within a community setting.
b. Demonstrate the ability to recognize and engage in learning opportunities prompted by interpersonal tensions within a small community or group setting.
c. Demonstrate the ability to listen to and interpret community needs that enrich my vocation to serve.

d. Demonstrate the ability to establish a sense of communal identity and belonging supportive of my vocation.

e. Demonstrate the ability to seek community settings that challenge my personal biases, behaviors, and relational deficiencies.

B. Objectives related to Ministry Engagement

9. Recognize contributions to implementing pastoral planning processes within the assigned ministries (P).

a. Demonstrate the ability to understand and promote parish goals and objectives (or mission-vision) within the assigned ministries.

b. Demonstrate the ability to engage in ministry planning and doing (project management).

c. Demonstrate the ability to articulate and provide examples of attitudes and behaviors that align with parish goals and objectives (or mission-vision)

10. Recognize the processes needed to conduct effective meetings (H, P).

References to the dimensions of formation:
I = Intellectual
H = Human
S = Spiritual
P = Pastoral

a. Demonstrate the ability to plan and manage effective meetings and apply consensus-seeking skills within any assigned ministries.

b. Demonstrate the ability to fulfill task commitments and meet deadlines that emerge from meetings (procrastination avoidance).

c. Demonstrate the ability to prevent ministry meetings from becoming just "business" meetings.

11. Recognize the value of cooperation and collaboration in parish ministry (H, P)

a. Demonstrate the ability to encourage others to be creative, resourceful, and engaging in tasks that need to be completed within any assigned ministries.
b. Demonstrate the ability to recognize that sometimes too much competition is a barrier to creating a sense of community (polarization).
c. Demonstrate the ability to articulate and provide examples of collaborative attitudes and behaviors.

12. Recognize the fundamentals of communicating to large groups (H, I, P).

a. Demonstrate the ability to use various techniques to offer effective presentations to ministry groups and large audiences in at least one of his assigned ministries.
b. Demonstrate the ability to use the variety of parish communications media as a tool for Evangelization.
c. Demonstrate the ability to objectively evaluate learning from presentation experiences to ministry groups and large audiences.
d. Demonstrate the ability to manage disinformation and unrealistic expectations.

13. Recognize the needs of the marginalized and the parish's role in providing relief (H, S, P).

References to the
dimensions of formation:
I = Intellectual
H = Human
S = Spiritual
P = Pastoral

a. Demonstrate the ability to seek and properly engage those parishioners on the fringes of participation in parish life.
b. Demonstrate the ability to encourage others to engage the poor and marginalized along with organizations or institutions already collaborating with the parish.

14. Recognize social justice needs, especially for the oppressed and discriminated (H, S, I, P).

a. Demonstrate the ability to correctly identify injustices and participate in activities that foster the human person's justice and dignity within the context of the assigned ministries.
b. Demonstrate the ability to defend the marginalized with words and actions consistent with Catholic Teaching.

15. Recognize the importance of offering religious instruction as Evangelization (H, I, P).

a. Demonstrate the ability to effectively offer a variety of classroom instruction on religion to different age groups.
b. Demonstrate the ability to reach out and persuade inactive parishioners or those far or fallen from the faith.
c. Demonstrate the ability to be a valuable resource for parish workshops, retreats, and/or days of reflection.

16. Recognize the relevance of conducting activities that foster a true community (Communion). (S, P)

a. Demonstrate the ability to exercise effective relational skills that enhance forming community in at least one of the assigned ministries.
b. Demonstrate the ability to identify and reduce barriers to forming a community.
c. Demonstrate the ability to differentiate between "organization" and "community" and pursue community-building objectives.

17. Recognize specialized pastoral needs of individuals, marriages, families, and parish ministry groups (H, S, P).

References to the
dimensions of formation:
I = Intellectual
H = Human
S = Spiritual
P = Pastoral

a. Demonstrate the ability to minister to situations of grief, aging, addiction, divorce, family dysfunctions, sexual orientation issues, and other exceptional cases that may be present in the assigned ministry.
b. Demonstrate the ability to recognize the value and engage in ministry beyond the parish setting (e.g., prison, hospital, food pantry, etc.)
c. Demonstrate the ability to awaken in others a pastoral sensitivity towards individuals with specialized needs.

18. Recognize the value of faith sharing and discernment in a ministry setting (H, S, P).

a. Demonstrate the ability to lead others in faith sharing and discernment processes when the opportunity arises in any assigned ministries.
b. Demonstrate the ability to Evangelize in prayer, service, and special interest groups and committees.
c. Demonstrate the ability to instruct persons or groups in using discernment practices.

C. Objectives related to Judgment and Decision making

19. Recognizes the need to maintain harmony between parish ministries and diocesan commitments (P).

a. Demonstrate the ability to balance the academic, human, spiritual, and pastoral capacities while assigned to the parish.
b. Demonstrate the ability to prioritize between the parish and diocesan events.
c. Demonstrate the ability to resolve conflicts between the parish and diocesan events.

20. Recognize situations where the ministry of presence is the most valuable pastoral response (H, S, P).

a. Demonstrate initiative in finding opportunities to be available to others and respond with pastoral presence.
b. Demonstrate the ability to recognize when listening skills are a sufficient pastoral response.
c. Demonstrate the ability to discern group or ministry activity situations where more experienced clergy may be required.

21. Recognize processes of conflict management, problem-solving, and decision-making H, P).

a. Demonstrate the ability to negotiate, diagnose, and formulate solutions to issues that emerge within an assigned ministry.
b. Demonstrate the ability to deal with conflicts within and among ministries.
c. Demonstrate the ability to navigate within the ambiguities that emerge in parish life.

References to the
dimensions of formation:
I = Intellectual
H = Human
S = Spiritual
P = Pastoral

d. Demonstrate the ability to detect and work with various pastoral situations and resources to address diverse moral and ethical concerns in parish life.

22. Recognize fundamentals of listening and interpersonal communications (H, S, P).

a. Demonstrate the ability to listen empathically and provide appropriate feedback in any of the assigned ministry settings.
b. Demonstrate the ability to interpret non-verbal cues of interpersonal communications.
c. Demonstrate the ability to recognize and resolve conflicting non-verbal and verbal cues.

23. Recognize the need to maintain confidentiality when required (H, S, P).

a. Demonstrate the ability to avoid disclosing among unconcerned persons any parishioner, ministry, or parish sensitive information.
b. Demonstrate the ability to discern the circumstances when the law requires to disclose information that may be confidential.
c. Demonstrate the ability to recognize when the disclosure type is more appropriate for the Sacrament of Reconciliation.

D. Objectives related to Pastoral Awareness

24. Recognize the influence of pastoral leadership in parish life (H, P).

> References to the
> dimensions of formation:
>   I = Intellectual
>   H = Human
>   S = Spiritual
>   P = Pastoral

a. Demonstrate the ability to recognize, develop, and exercise a personal style of pastoral leadership that fosters team building and mutuality in ministry.
b. Demonstrate the ability to incorporate spiritual discernment in the exercise of ministry leadership roles.
c. Demonstrate a pastoral leadership style that is rooted in the uniqueness of personal vocation.

25. Recognizes the cycles of parish life and its relevance to pastoral practice (H, P).

a. Demonstrate the ability to relate parish demographics to increases and decreases of the pastoral workload.
b. Demonstrate the ability to plan pastoral activities that address contingencies, stress, or trauma in parish life (e.g., pastor transitions, mergers, closings, etc.)
c. Demonstrate the ability to design and implement pastoral activities that address contingencies, stress, or trauma in parish life (e.g., pastor transitions, mergers, closings, etc.)

26. Recognize the value the principles of Stewardship applied to parish life (P).

a. Demonstrate the ability to recognize and promote the principles of parish stewardship.
b. Demonstrate the ability to articulate the connection between parish stewardship objectives and parish and diocesan support.
c. Demonstrate the ability to deliver a witness on the value of Stewardship.

27. Recognize the contributions of parish employment management and human resources (Parish Staff) (H, S, I, P)

References to the
dimensions of formation:
I = Intellectual
H = Human
S = Spiritual
P = Pastoral

a. Demonstrate the ability to cooperate seamlessly with parish staff and supporting volunteers.
b. Demonstrate the ability to relate the archdiocesan / diocesan employee manual to the potential and challenges of pastoral ministry.
c. Demonstrate pastoral sensitivity and appreciation when dealing with volunteers and volunteer groups supporting the parish.
d. Demonstrate the ability to understand and comply with the archdiocesan /diocesan guidelines to protect the vulnerable.

28. Recognize the value of prayer and reflection in dealing with parish life (H, S, P).

a. Demonstrate the ability to engage self and others in prayer and reflection, individually and in group settings.
b. Demonstrate the ability to take the initiative to offer introductory reflections and prayers at the beginning or end of ministry meetings attended.
c. Demonstrate the ability to foster and conduct discernment processes for individuals and in group settings.

29. Recognize the laity's evolving roles, leadership, and responsibilities (H, I, P).

a. Demonstrate the ability to work with a diversity of lay roles and responsibilities in ministry, liturgies, and sacramental preparation.
b. Demonstrate the ability to encourage and conduct lay leadership development activities.

c. Demonstrate the ability to provide constructive feedback in situations where lay functioning may be too distracting or disruptive.

d. Demonstrate the ability to encourage the laity to realize and pursue their vocations and apostolate duties.

30. Recognize a variety of institutions and organizations supportive of parish life (H, P).

a. Familiarization with local non-profit and government programs designed to support parishioner needs.

b. Demonstrate the ability to access and use various parish, parish and diocesan, and diocesan resources to promote and fulfill goals on objectives within any assigned ministries.

References to the dimensions of formation:
I = Intellectual
H = Human
S = Spiritual
P = Pastoral

31. Recognize the pastoral implications of health, safety, and security (H, I, P).

a. Demonstrate the ability to evaluate distracting or disruptive issues of facilities maintenance and repairs.

b. Demonstrate the ability to identify and raise safety and security concerns.

c. Demonstrate the ability to interface with contracted and organic temporalities services in the parish.

32. Recognize and value the contribution of women to church leadership and parish life (H, I, P).

a. Demonstrate the ability to manage personal attitudes and perceived threats of women in ministry.
b. Demonstrate the ability to address cultural inequities and biases related to the vocation and gifts of women.
c. Demonstrate the ability to foster the contributions and gifts of women in parish life.

33. Recognize the value of balancing pastoral sensitivity and doctrinal disagreements in parish life (H, I, P)
Insert image 6

a. Demonstrate knowledge of current issues affecting the proper understanding of Church doctrine.
b. Demonstrate the ability to argue for Church doctrine while maintaining pastoral sensitivity.
c. Demonstrate application of healthy coping skills when dealing with pastoral pressures.

PARTE 2 - OBJETIVOS Y METAS ESENCIALES

El Panorama de Aprendizaje Pastoral

PARTE 2

Objetivos y Metas Esenciales

Esta segunda parte del manual presenta los objetivos esenciales del aprendizaje pastoral parroquial en cuatro secciones, a saber, los objetivos relacionados con: (a) el desarrollo de la vocación, (b) la participación en el ministerio, (c) el juicio y la toma de decisiones, y (d) la sensibilidad pastoral. Cada uno de los objetivos dentro de estas secciones tiene objetivos más específicos. Vale la pena señalar que la mayoría de los objetivos y metas no están directamente asociados con ningún ministerio parroquial en particular, lo que permite al aprendiz pastoral la flexibilidad de elegir el ministerio más apropiado en función de lo que la parroquia asignada pueda ofrecer. Así, por ejemplo, Objetivo 9 *"Reconocer los procesos necesarios para llevar a cabo reuniones efectivas"* puede ser aplicado al Ministerio de la Juventud, así como a las reuniones del Grupo de Oración. Cada objetivo y los objetivos subsiguientes se diseñaron para permitir la flexibilidad en la selección de la estructura del ministerio.

A. Objetivos relacionados con el desarrollo de la vocación

1. Reconoce el valor de recibir sugerencias de otros (H, P).

a. Demostrar que acepta ideas y sugerencias del Párroco.

b. Demostrar que acepta ideas de compañeros o mentores en sesiones de grupos pequeños.

c. Demostrar la capacidad de realizar autoevaluaciones e identificar eventos clave de aprendizaje dentro de los ministerios asignados.

2. Reconoce la importancia de articular las experiencias pastorales en el contexto del crecimiento personal (H, P).

a. Demostrar la capacidad de integrar el aprendizaje pastoral en el contexto general de su formación.
b. Demostrar la capacidad de articular el aprendizaje pastoral para su párroco, formadores y/o grupos de mentores.

3. Reconocer los efectos de las experiencias pastorales en la profundización de la madurez personal en la fe (S, P).

a. Demostrar la capacidad de buscar y cumplir objetivos pastorales que son lo suficientemente desafiantes para promover crecimiento y madurez en la fe.
b. Demostrar la capacidad de desarrollar una actitud madura y humilde usando como plataforma un ministerio parroquial asignado.

4. Reconocer la necesidad de tomar iniciativas dentro de las capacidades y limitaciones propias (H, P).

a. Demostrar la capacidad de discernir las necesidades pastorales de al menos uno de los ministerios asignados y ofrecer soluciones realistas y de valor añadido.
b. Demostrar la capacidad de discernir fronteras de interacción con otros y reconocer, cuando necesario, la intervención de profesionales.
c. Demostrar la capacidad de aplicar efectivamente las destrezas constructivas de afrontamiento cuando ocurren grandes tensiones y presiones en un ministerio de la parroquia.

5. Reconocer la importancia de seguir el acuerdo de aprendizaje pastoral (H, S, I).

a. Demostrar la capacidad de seleccionar, planificar y cumplir los objetivos de aprendizaje pastoral acordados.

b. Demostrar la capacidad de reconocer seleccionar objetivos valiosos y realizables, y presentar recomendaciones o cambios si los objetivos no son realistas (demasiado fáciles, demasiado difíciles).

6. Reconocer cómo las actitudes, valores y prejuicios personales afectan al ministerio pastoral (H, P).

a. Demostrar la capacidad de estar a la disposición de los demás mientras se mantienen las fronteras interpersonales adecuadas.
b. Demostrar la capacidad de identificar y manejar los prejuicios personales que pueden limitar la efectividad pastoral.
c. Demostrar la capacidad de buscar oportunidades y situaciones que permitan evaluar los progresos en el manejo de prejuicios.

7. Reconocer que obras de ministerio fluye de los dones propios y el discernimiento vocacional (S, P).

a. Demostrar la capacidad de identificar y participar en actividades ministeriales que fomentan y desafían los carismas personales y la búsqueda vocacional.
b. Demostrar la capacidad de articular los efectos del aprendizaje pastoral dentro del contexto de la vocación.

8. Reconocer el valor de participar activamente en vida comunitaria como parte del crecimiento personal (P).

a. Demostrar la capacidad de experimentar y compartir alegremente con otros dentro de un entorno comunitario.

b. Demostrar la capacidad de reconocer y participar en oportunidades de aprendizaje impulsadas por tensiones interpersonales dentro de una comunidad pequeña o un entorno grupal.

c. Demostrar la capacidad de escuchar e interpretar necesidades de la comunidad que enriquecen mi vocación al servicio.

d. Demostrar la capacidad de establecer un sentido de identidad comunitaria y pertenencia que apoye mi vocación.

e. Demostrar la capacidad de buscar entornos comunitarios que desafíen mis prejuicios, comportamientos, y deficiencias sociales.

B. Objetivos relacionados con la participación del Ministerio

9. Reconocer las contribuciones y la aplicación de los procesos de planificación pastoral (P).

a. Demostrar la capacidad de comprender y promover objetivos y metas parroquiales (o visión de misión) dentro de los ministerios asignados.

b. Demostrar la capacidad de participar en la planificación y la realización de proyectos en los ministerios asignados (gestión de proyectos).

c. Demostrar la capacidad de articular y dar ejemplos de actitudes y comportamientos que se ajustan a objetivos y metas parroquiales (o visión de misión).

10. Reconocer los procesos necesarios para conducir reuniones (juntas) eficaces (H, P).

a. Demostrar la capacidad de planificar y gestionar reuniones eficaces y aplicar las aptitudes para la búsqueda de consenso en los ministerios asignados.
b. Demostrar la capacidad de cumplir los compromisos de tareas y plazos que surgen de las reuniones (evitar las dilaciones).
c. Demostrar la capacidad de evitar que las reuniones del ministerio se conviertan en simples reuniones de "negocios".

11. Reconocer el valor de la cooperación y colaboración en el ministerio de la parroquia (H, P).

a. Demostrar la capacidad de alentar a otros a ser creativos, ingeniosos y participar en tareas asignadas dentro de un ministerio asignado.
b. Demostrar la capacidad de reconocer que a veces demasiada competencia es una barrera para crear un sentido de comunidad (Comunión).
c. Demostrar la capacidad de articular y dar ejemplos de actitudes y comportamientos colaborativos.

12. Reconocer los fundamentos de la comunicación en grandes grupos (H, I, P).

a. Demostrar la capacidad de usar diversas técnicas para ofrecer presentaciones efectivas a grupos ministeriales y grandes audiencias en al menos uno de sus ministerios asignados.
b. Demostrar la capacidad de usar la variedad de medios de comunicación parroquiales como herramienta para la evangelización.

c. Demostrar la capacidad de evaluar objetivamente y aprender de las experiencias de presentación a grupos ministeriales y grandes audiencias.

13. Reconocer las necesidades de los marginados y el rol de la parroquia en ofrecer ayudas apropiadas (H, S, P)

a. Demostrar la capacidad de buscar y promover la integración de esos feligreses que están en los márgenes de las actividades parroquiales.
b. Demostrar la capacidad de alentar a otros a que se involucren con las organizaciones o instituciones dedicados a pobres y marginadas.

14. Reconocer las necesidades de la justicia social, especialmente para los oprimidos y discriminados (H, S, I, P).

a. Demostrar la capacidad de captar y expresar adecuadamente las injusticias, y participar en actividades que fomenten la justicia y la dignidad de la persona humana en el contexto de los ministerios designados.
b. Demostrar la capacidad de defender a los marginados con palabras y acciones consistentes con la enseñanza católica.

15. Reconocer la importancia de ofrecer instrucción religiosa como Evangelización (H, I, P).

a. Demostrar la capacidad de ofrecer efectivamente una variedad de clases sobre religión a grupos de diferentes edades o culturas.
b. Demostrar la capacidad de alcanzar y persuadir a los feligreses inactivos o a aquellos que están lejos o han caído lejos de la fe.
c. Demostrar la habilidad de ser un recurso valioso para talleres parroquiales, retiros y/o días de reflexión.

16. Reconocer la necesidad de realizar actividades que fomenten una verdadera comunidad (Comunión) (S, P).

a. Demostrar la capacidad de ejercer destrezas interpersonales efectivas que mejoren la formación de comunidades en al menos uno de los ministerios asignados.
b. Demostrar la capacidad de identificar y reducir las barreras para formar pequeñas comunidades.
c. Demostrar la capacidad de diferenciar entre "organización" y "comunidad" y perseguir objetivos para construcción un sentido sano de comunidad.

17. Reconocer las necesidades pastorales especializadas de personas, matrimonios, familias y grupos (H, S, P).

a. Demostrar la capacidad de ministrar situaciones de dolor, depresión, adicción, divorcio, disfunciones familiares, temas de orientación sexual y otros casos excepcionales.
b. Demostrar la capacidad de reconocer el valor y participar en el ministerio más allá del entorno de la parroquia (por ejemplo, prisión, hospital, despensa de alimentos, etc.)
c. Demostrar la capacidad de despertar en otros una sensibilidad pastoral hacia individuos con necesidades especializadas.

18. Reconocer el valor del compartir la fe y el discernimiento en un contexto ministerial (H, S, P).

a. Demostrar la capacidad de dirigir a otros en procesos de intercambio de creencias y discernimiento cuando se presenta la oportunidad en cualquier ministerio asignado.

b. Demostrar la capacidad de evangelizar en oración, servicio y mediante grupos o comités de intereses especiales.

c. Demostrar la capacidad de instruir a personas o grupos en el uso del discernimiento.

C. Objetivos de juicio y adopción de decisiones

19. Reconocer la necesidad de mantener la armonía entre los ministerios parroquiales y los compromisos con el seminario y la diócesis (P).

a. Demostrar la capacidad de equilibrar las capacidades académicas, humanas, espirituales y pastorales mientras asignado a la parroquia.

b. Demostrar la capacidad de priorizar entre los eventos parroquiales y diocesanos.

c. Demostrar la capacidad de resolver conflictos entre eventos parroquiales y diocesanos.

20. Reconocer situaciones donde el ministerio de presencia es la respuesta pastoral más valiosa (H, S, P).

a. Demostrar iniciativa en la búsqueda de oportunidades para estar a disposición de otros y responder con presencia pastoral.

b. Demostrar la capacidad de reconocer cuando las habilidades de escucha son una respuesta pastoral suficiente.

c. Demostrar la capacidad de discernir situaciones individuales o en grupo en las que puede ser necesario un miembro del clero más experimentado.

21. Reconocer los procesos de manejo de conflictos, resolución de problemas y toma de decisiones (H, P).

a. Demostrar la capacidad de negociar, diagnosticar y formular soluciones a los conflictos que surgen dentro de un ministerio asignado.
b. Demostrar la capacidad de lidiar con los conflictos entre grupos ministeriales.
c. Demostrar la capacidad de navegar dentro de las ambigüedades que surgen en la vida parroquial.
d. Demostrar la capacidad de detectar y trabajar con una variedad de situaciones y recursos pastorales que retan diversas temas morales y éticas.

22. Reconocer las habilidades de escuchar en las comunicaciones interpersonales (H, S, P).

a. Demostrar la capacidad de escuchar empáticamente y proporcionar sugerencias apropiadas.
b. Demostrar la capacidad de interpretar las señales no verbales en comunicaciones interpersonales.
c. Demostrar la capacidad de reconocer y resolver contradicciones entre señales no verbales y verbales.

23. Reconocer la necesidad de mantener confidencialidad (H, S, P).

a. Demostrar la capacidad de evitar revelar cualquier información delicada o sensitiva relacionado con feligreses, ministerios o la parroquia.
b. Demostrar la capacidad de discernir las circunstancias cuando la ley exige revelar información que de otra manera sería confidencial.

c. Demostrar la capacidad de reconocer cuando el tipo de divulgación personal es más apropiado para el Sacramento de la Reconciliación.

D. Objetivos relacionados con la conciencia pastoral

24. Reconocer la influencia del liderazgo pastoral en la vida parroquial (H, P).

a. Demostrar la capacidad de reconocer, desarrollar y ejercer un estilo personal de liderazgo pastoral que fomente sanas dinámicas de grupos y pequeñas comunidades.
b. Demostrar la capacidad de incorporar el discernimiento espiritual en el ejercicio de los roles de liderazgo del ministerio.
c. Demostrar un estilo de liderazgo pastoral que se basa en la originalidad de la vocación personal.

25. Reconoce los ciclos de vida parroquial y su importancia para la práctica pastoral (H, P).

a. Demostrar la capacidad de relacionar datos demográficos de la parroquia con sus posibles aumentos y disminuciones de la carga de trabajo pastoral.
b. Demostrar la capacidad de diseñar y planificar actividades pastorales que aborden contingencias, estrés o trauma en la vida parroquial (por ejemplo, transiciones de pastores, fusiones, cierres, etc.)
c. Demostrar la capacidad de implementar actividades pastorales que aborden contingencias, estrés o trauma en la vida parroquial (por ejemplo, transiciones de pastores, fusiones, cierres, etc.)

26. Reconocer el valor de los principios de administración aplicados a la vida de parroquia (P).

a. Demostrar la capacidad de reconocer y promover las funciones operacionales en la administración parroquial.
b. Demostrar la capacidad de articular la conexión entre los objetivos de la administración parroquial y el desarrollo pastoral.
c. Demostrar la capacidad de reconocer el valor de la Administración parroquial.

27. Reconocer las contribuciones de la gestión parroquial del empleo y de los recursos humanos (personal parroquial ((H, S, I, P).

a. Demostrar la capacidad de cooperar sin problemas con el personal de parroquia y apoyar a los voluntarios.
b. Demostrar la capacidad de relacionar el manual de los empleados arquidiocesanos / diocesanos con el potencial y los desafíos del ministerio pastoral.
c. Demostrar sensibilidad pastoral y aprecio al tratar con voluntarios y grupos de voluntarios que apoyan a la parroquia.
d. Demostrar la capacidad de comprender y cumplir las directrices arquidiocesanos o diocesanos para proteger a los vulnerables.

28. Reconocer el valor de la oración y la reflexión en el manejo de la vida parroquial (H, S, P).

a. Demostrar la habilidad de involucrarse y a los demás en la oración y la reflexión, individualmente y en grupos.
b. Demostrar la capacidad de tomar la iniciativa de ofrecer reflexiones introductorias y oraciones al comienzo o al final de las reuniones ministeriales.

c. Demostrar la capacidad de fomentar y llevar a cabo procesos de discernimiento para individuos y en grupos.

29. Reconocer la evolución de los roles, el liderazgo y las responsabilidades del laico (H, I, P).

a. Demostrar la capacidad de trabajar con una diversidad de roles y responsabilidades laicos en el ministerio, liturgias y preparación sacramental.

b. Demostrar la capacidad de alentar y llevar a cabo actividades de desarrollo del liderazgo en ministerios.

c. Demostrar la capacidad de proporcionar retroalimentación constructiva en situaciones donde la contribución de un laico es inapropiada.

30. Reconocer una variedad de instituciones y organizaciones que apoyan la vida parroquial (H, P).

a. Familiarización con programas locales sin fines de lucro y gubernamentales diseñados para apoyar las necesidades de los feligreses.

b. Demostrar la capacidad de acezar y utilizar diversos recursos parroquiales, parroquiales, diocesanos y diocesanos para promover y cumplir los objetivos en cualquiera de los ministerios asignados.

31. Reconocer las implicaciones pastorales de la salud, la seguridad y la protección (H, I, P).

a. Demostrar la capacidad de evaluar los problemas de infraestructura que distraen o perturban los procesos de desarrollo pastoral.

b. Demostrar la capacidad de identificar y plantear problemas de seguridad.

c. Demostrar la capacidad de interactuar con servicios de temporalidades innatas a la parroquia y servicios contratadas para la parroquia.

32. Reconocer y valorar la contribución de las mujeres al liderazgo de la iglesia y la vida parroquial (H, I, P).

a. Demostrar la capacidad de manejar las actitudes personales y las amenazas percibidas de las mujeres en el ministerio.

b. Demostrar la capacidad de abordar las desigualdades culturales y los prejuicios relacionados con la vocación y los dones de las mujeres.

c. Demostrar la capacidad de fomentar las contribuciones y los dones de las mujeres en la vida parroquial.

33. Reconocer el valor de equilibrar la sensibilidad pastoral con desacuerdos doctrinales en la vida parroquial (H, I, P).

a. Demostrar conocimiento de los problemas actuales que afectan la comprensión correcta de la doctrina de la Iglesia.

b. Demostrar la capacidad de defender la doctrina de la Iglesia mientras se mantiene sensibilidad pastoral hacia el otro.

c. Demostrar la aplicación de habilidades para sobrellevar y adaptarse a las presiones pastorales.

PART 3 - DIACONATE OBJECTIVES AND GOALS

The Landscape of Pastoral Learning

PART 3

Diaconate Objectives and Goals

In addition to the previously presented landscape for learning the essentials of parish life, there are specific objectives and goals for the diaconate. An assumption is that upon ordination to the diaconate, the learner has a well-rounded understanding of parish life. Therefore, the objectives for the diaconate can focus more on aims commensurate with his status as a member of the clergy.

Objectives Specific Goals

Objectives	Specific Goals
1. Recognize the sacramental and liturgical roles of the deacon.	a. Demonstrate the ability to adequately prepare for a variety of sacraments and liturgies. b. Demonstrate deep reverence in the performance of sacramental and liturgical functions. c. Demonstrate the ability to deliver homilies and reflections commensurate with the attendees' intellectual, emotional, social, and spiritual standing.
2. Recognizes pastoral leadership as a key dimension of pastoral maturation.	a. Demonstrate the ability to recognize, develop, and exercise a personal style of pastoral leadership that fosters team building and mutuality. b. Demonstrate the ability to assume leadership roles within complex pastoral situations present in the assigned ministry.

c. Demonstrate the ability to recognize the value and engage in ministry beyond just the parish setting (e.g., prison, hospital, food pantry, etc.).

d. Demonstrate the ability to perceive, suggest, and implement improvements in the quality of pastoral competencies within the parish setting.

3. Recognize the relevance of pastoral sensitivity as an ordained minister.

a. Demonstrate the ability to express love and care when providing comfort to those that are hurting and in need.

b. Demonstrate the ability to empathize with the variety of attendee moods before and after sacraments and liturgies (e.g., weddings, funerals, baptisms).

c. Demonstrate the ability to resist speaking or saying something profound with an expectation of eliminating grief by his insight.

d. Demonstrate the ability to discern situations where more experienced clergy is required.

e. Demonstrate an attitude of unity and fellowship when sharing with individuals and communities of other faiths (inter-religious).

4. Recognize the significance of continued personal growth as an ordained minister.

a. Demonstrate the ability to discern and engage in pastoral and liturgical activities that challenge and nurture his personal gifts and vocational path.

b. Demonstrate the ability to continue to make discoveries along the dimensions of formation into his life and ministry.

c. Demonstrate the ability to integrate pastoral learning experiences within the overall context of the next steps in the growth of his vocational awareness.

b. Demonstrate the ability to articulate the implications of ongoing pastoral learning in a group setting (face to face or virtually).

5. Recognize Evangelization as a quintessential activity of the diaconate experience.

a. Demonstrate the ability to Evangelize in prayer, service, and special interest groups and committees.

b. Demonstrate the ability to offer various classroom instruction on religious topics to different age and cultural groups.

c. Demonstrate the ability to identify and engage in opportunities to assist the marginalized within the parish and the local community.

d. Demonstrate the ability to carry out pastoral work collaboratively with others and an appreciation for the different charisms and vocations within the Church.

e. Demonstrate the ability to actively participate in community outreach activities that promote equality for cultural differences, ethnicities, and the socially oppressed.

Ronald R. Rojas

6. Recognizes the need to maintain harmony between parish support and diocesan commitments.

a. Demonstrate the ability to balance the academic, human, spiritual, and ministerial workloads while engaged in diocesan and outreach activities.
b. Demonstrate the ability to prioritize between the parish and diocesan community activities.
c. Demonstrate the ability to plan and perform to a parish work schedule with minimal conflicts with diocesan activities.

PARTE 4 - OBJETIVOS Y METAS PARA EL DIACONADO

El Panorama de Aprendizaje Pastoral

PARTE 4

Objetivos y metas para el diaconado

Además del panorama previamente presentado para aprender lo esencial de la vida parroquial, existen objetivos y metas específicas para el diaconado. Una suposición es que, al ordenarse al diaconado, el aprendiz ya posea una comprensión abarcadora de vida parroquial. Así los objetivos para el diaconado pueden centrarse más en aspectos acordes con su condición de miembro del clero.

Objetivos Objetivos específicos

1. Reconocer los roles sacramentales y litúrgicos del diácono.

a. Demostrar la capacidad de prepararse adecuadamente para una variedad de sacramentos y liturgias.
b. Demostrar profunda reverencia en el desempeño de funciones sacramentales y litúrgicas.
c. Demostrar la capacidad de ofrecer homilías y reflexiones proporcionales a la realidad intelectual, emocional, social y espiritual de los asistentes.

2. Reconocer que el liderazgo pastoral es una dimensión clave de la maduración pastoral

a. Demostrar la capacidad de reconocer, desarrollar y ejercer un estilo personal de liderazgo pastoral que fomente la creación de equipos y la mutualidad.
b. Demostrar la capacidad de asumir funciones de liderazgo en situaciones pastorales complejas en el ministerio asignado.

c. Demostrar la capacidad de reconocer el valor y participar en el ministerio más allá del entorno parroquial (por ejemplo, prisión, hospital, despensa de alimentos, etc.).

d. Demostrar la capacidad de percibir, sugerir e implementar mejoras en la calidad de las competencias pastorales dentro del entorno de la parroquia.

3. Reconocer la relevancia de la sensibilidad pastoral como ministro ordenado.

a. Demostrar la capacidad de expresar amor y cuidado cuando se proporciona consuelo a los que sufren y necesitan.

b. Demostrar la capacidad de empatizar correspondientemente a la variedad de estados de ánimo antes y después de los sacramentos y liturgias (por ejemplo, bodas, funerales, bautismos).

c. Demostrar la capacidad de resistir hablar o sugerir soluciones perspicaces con la esperanza de eliminar el dolor.

d. Demostrar la capacidad de discernir situaciones en las que se requiere un clero más experimentado.

e. Demostrar una actitud de unidad y compañerismo cuando se comparte con personas y comunidades de otras religiones (interreligiosas).

4. Reconocer la importancia de un crecimiento personal continuo como ministro ordenado.

a. Demostrar la capacidad de discernir y participar en actividades pastorales y litúrgicas que desafían y alimentan sus dones personales y la trayectoria sacerdotal.

b. Demostrar la capacidad de seguir haciendo descubrimientos a lo largo de las dimensiones de la formación en su vida y ministerio.

c. Demostrar la capacidad de integrar las experiencias de aprendizaje pastoral en el contexto general de los próximos pasos hacia la vocación sacerdotal.

d. Demostrar la capacidad de articular apropiadamente y en foro público las experiencias de aprendizaje pastoral.

5. Reconocer la evangelización como una actividad primordial de la experiencia diaconal.

a. Demostrar la capacidad de evangelizar en oración, servicio, en grupos y comités de interés especiales.

b. Demostrar la capacidad de ofrecer una variedad de instrucción en aula de temas religiosos a diferentes edades y grupos culturales.

c. Demostrar la capacidad de identificar y aprovechar oportunidades para ayudar a los marginados dentro de la parroquia y la comunidad local.

d. Demostrar la capacidad de realizar una labor pastoral en colaboración con otros y apreciar los diferentes carismas y vocaciones dentro de la Iglesia.

e. Demostrar la capacidad de participar activamente en actividades que promuevan la igualdad en las diferencias culturales, étnicas y grupos socialmente oprimidas.

6. Reconoce la necesidad de mantener la armonía entre el apoyo parroquial y los compromisos con el seminario y la diócesis.

a. Demostrar la capacidad de equilibrar las cargas de trabajo académicas, humanas, espirituales y pastorales mientras se dedican a actividades diocesanas y del seminario.

b. Demostrar la capacidad de priorizar entre las actividades de parroquia y las de la comunidad diocesana.

c. Demostrar la capacidad de planificar y realizar un programa de trabajo parroquial con un mínimo de conflictos con actividades diocesanas.

PART 5 - ADMINISTRATION IN PARISH LIFE

The Landscape of Pastoral Learning

Course Syllabus for Parish Administration
(With suggested assignments and KSAs for each key topic)

PART 5

Administration in Parish Life

This syllabus is a structured presentation of the roles and responsibilities of a parish administrator (pastor) in syllabus format. Below is the schedule of planned topics and the learning objectives, suggested assignments (in English and Spanish), and the Knowledge, Skills, and Abilities (KSA) corresponding to each case. The syllabus is configured for a 13-week semester.

The syllabus also serves as guidance, even if a specific course on pastoral leadership is unavailable. In aligning with this handbook's objective, it offers a comprehensive view of parish leadership responsibilities with the intent of providing an initial exposure to topics that otherwise may be missed during a more advanced experiencing of parish life. Many of these topics, especially those related to parish operations—such as Human Resources, Finances, Temporalities, and Stewardship—take time to absorb. Yet being able to become familiar with these topics allows the seminarian the opportunity to grow into these aspects of parish life and somewhat moderate the "trauma" of having to go through a "crash course on how to become an administrator years later in their vocation.

This course provides topical lectures, case studies, guest speakers, student discussion, and self-assessments to prepare the seminarian for the role of parish leadership as it relates to proper and effective management and administration of a parish. This suggested course explores critical issues that pastors and administrators will face. Seminarians will discuss a variety of ways to approach both effective management and problem-solving techniques. The course employs a practical approach that seeks to help the seminarian understand the role of the Administrator-Pastor as Manager and how it relates to his other responsibilities associated with parish life. The variety of assignments during the course are intended to expose the seminarian to a deeper appreciation of parish life. It will also help the seminarian think strategically about the leadership of a parish within the priestly vocation.

Date	Topic	Learning Objectives
Week 1	Foundations of Pastoral Leadership and Administration (Ch1,2)	a. Developing awareness of the influence of secularly generated leadership and management models in parish life and parish administration. b. Rooting administrative leadership roles as another step as the vocation evolves (priestly identity). c. Review models of secular administrator-leadership and view Pastoral Leadership-Administration as a spiritual practice. *M1 Assignment Paper:* *Describe why it is essential to root your pastoral leadership style (as an eventual Administrator) within your vocation and describe some of the major opposing forces you think you may encounter during your leadership maturation process (during the next 6-8 years). Write a 5-7 paragraph personal reflective and send this assignment as an email to the instructor. This assignment does not require any specific formatting or addition of supporting sources since it is more a personal reflective than a scholarly submission. What matters for this assignment is expressing how well you can relate leadership to your vocation's growth (100pts).* *(Note: If you find it easier to express yourself in Spanish, it is acceptable. What matters is that you can reflect on the relationship between leadership and your vocation.)*

		Explique por qué es esencial comprender el liderazgo pastoral en el contexto de la vocación personal y describe algunas de las fuerzas que pueden oponerse a que madure su propio crecimiento como líder (piense sobre los próximos 6-8 años). Escriba un ensayo reflexionando sobre este tema y envíelo como email a su instructor. Esta tarea no requiere el uso de fuentes académicas, ni tampoco requiere formato específico. Lo que es significativo es que pueda expresar plenamente la relación del ser líder (dirigente) con su vocación. (100 puntos). *Topic 1: Knowledge, Skills, and Abilities (KSA)* *(K) Knowledge of the fundamentals of secular leadership theory and most common models.* *(S) Skill in rooting personal leadership practices from within the framework of a maturing priestly vocation.* *(A) Ability in recognizing secular model insufficiencies when applied to the parish environment.*
Week 2	Administering to the parish as a Faith Community (Ch 6)	a. Comprehend parish as *faith community* and review the parish (pastoral) council's roles as foundational to pastoral administration. b. Assess parish life using parish vitality indicators and understand its relationship to parish administration. c. Discuss the relevance of parish administration in protecting and guiding parish life (growth, transitions, mergers, closings, and trauma-healing)

			M2 Discussion Assignment:
			Review the "parish vitality indicators" and chart discussed in the chat and offer your perceptions on how well your current parish assignment would score. There is no need to collect actual data; just present an appreciation of what you know so far about your assigned parish. Review with an Administrator's (Pastor) perspective. What seems to be working well? What areas could use improvement? Summarize your perceptions and observations with 3-5 paragraphs and comment on at least two other postings (50 pts).
			(Note: If you would like the additional practice, its acceptable if your responses to other students are in Spanish)
			Repase los indicadores de vitalidad parroquial discutidos en clase y ofrece tu puntuación estimada. No es necesario coleccionar data específica, sino que se pide una apreciación estimada de la situación en tu parroquia asignada. Resume tus percepciones y observaciones en 3-5 párrafos y ofrece comentarios en las contestaciones de al menos dos otros estudiantes (50 puntos).
			Topic 2: Knowledge, Skills, and Abilities (KSA)
			(K) Knowledge of the difference between "organization" and "community" as it applies to the parish setting. *(S) Skill in adapting to transitions of pastors*
			(A) Ability to recognize needs and growth patterns in parish life.

| Week 3 | Evaluating parish charisms and faith-vision (Ch 7) | a. Understand the basics of social artifacts for a community envisioning process as a framework for pastoral administration. b. Differentiate corporate strategic planning and the staff's role in parish strategic discerning. c. Recognize various organizational artifacts to guide community life and its connection to administration and parish staff.

M3 Discussion Assignment:

Describe the charisms of the parish where you are currently assigned and conduct an analysis of the mission and vision of the parish-based on its charisms. What are the charisms of the parish? How are they reflected in the parish faith-vision and mission? How are they enacted and embodied in parish life? Write a 3-5 paragraph summary of your observations and respond to at least two other postings (50 pts).

(Note: If you would like the additional practice, its acceptable if your responses to other students are in Spanish)

Describe los carismas de la parroquia a la cual has sido asignado y conduce un análisis de la misión y visión parroquial usando los carismas como punto de contraste. ¿Cuáles son los carismas de la parroquia? ¿Cómo están reflejados en la misión y visión de la parroquia? ¿De qué maneras específicas se llevan a cabo esta misión y visión nen la vida parroquial? Resume tus percepciones y observaciones en 3-5 párrafos y ofrece comentarios en las contestaciones de al menos dos otros estudiantes (50 puntos). |
|--------|------|------|

		Topic 3: Knowledge, Skills, and Abilities (KSA) *K) Knowledge of the difference between corporate strategic planning and parish strategic discerning.* *(S) Skill in using social artifacts to inspire, unify and mobilize a parish community.* *(A) Ability to identify parish charisms and use them in pastoral work.*
Week 4	Controlling and accounting of financial resources	a. Understand the fundamentals of accounting of financial resources through budget formulation and financial reporting. b. See the value of maintaining sources of revenue beyond just Sunday collections. c. Appreciate the Finance Council's relevance and functions concerning parish administration and staff. *M4 Assignment Paper:* *For this assignment, obtain a copy of the parish budget (either current year or past year). Identify and describe 5 (five) specific techniques, methods, or practices you would use now and in the immediate future to assess a parish budget's effectiveness. What seems right? What seems odd? What do you expect? How are contingencies managed? Maybe you have other observations. Explain why you think the techniques you have chosen work best for you. Write and send as an email to the instructor. This assignment does not require any specific formatting since it is more a personal reflective than a scholarly submission (100 pts)*

		Para esta tarea es necesario obtener una copia del presupuesto de la parroquia (ya sea el presupuesto actual o uno anterior). Identifica y describe cinco (5) técnicas específicas que usarías personalmente para evaluar la efectividad de un presupuesto parroquial. Explique por qué piensas que para ti son las técnicas más efectivas. Conteste por escrito a tu instructor mediante email. Esta tarea no requiere formato específico ni fuentes académicas, ya que es más bien una reflexión personal (100 puntos). *Topic 4: Knowledge, Skills, and Abilities (KSA)* *(K) Knowledge of accounting, budgetary, and parish financial practices and procedures.* *(S) Skill in composing budgets and reviewing financial statements* *(A) Ability to manage a budget and work within the constraints of that budget.*
Week 5	Understanding parish business operations	a. Appreciate the functions and dynamics of parish staff operations concerning parish life. b. Summarize human development functions (HR) and their relevance to staff development. c. Relate to external (secular) parish supporting businesses and agencies. d. Review parish information systems. e. Become familiar with sacramental record keeping.

<table>
<tr><td></td><td></td><td>

M5 Discussion Assignment:

Two relevant groups that are available to the Administrator/Pastor to align and guide the pastoral (community) and the business (organization) efforts of the parish are the pastoral council and the parish staff. Ideally, their plans, objectives, and attitudes complement each other to the benefit of parish life. But naturally, there are synergies and tensions among these two groups. What are your impressions of the relationship between these two groups and their contribution to parish life in the parish you are currently assigned? Does the business operations of the parish have an Evangelization responsibility? How do you see it enacted? Offer your impressions in 3-5 paragraphs, and remember to respond or comment to at least two other postings (50 pts).

(Note: If you would like the additional practice, its acceptable if your responses to other students are in Spanish)

Dos grupos pertinentes a la conducción pastoral de la parroquia (vida comunitaria) y los aspectos comerciales de la parroquia son el consejo parroquial y el personal de la oficina. Idealmente, sus planes, objetivos y actitudes se complementan y están al servicio mutuo de la vida parroquial. Sin embargo, hay sinergias y tensiones entre estos dos grupos. ¿Cuáles son tus impresiones sobre la relación entre estos dos grupos y sus contribuciones a la vida parroquial en la parroquia a la cual estas actualmente asignado? Resume tus impresiones en 3-5 párrafos y ofrece comentarios en las contestaciones de al menos dos otros estudiantes (50 puntos).

</td></tr>
</table>

		Topic 5: Knowledge, Skills, and Abilities (KSA) *(K) Knowledge of basic parish staff organizational functions and information systems.* *(S) Skill in managing and supervising employees (full-time & part-time staff).* *(S) Skill in the use of standard office equipment and software.* *(A) Ability to work collaboratively and build positive relations with employees, peers, volunteers, and contractors.* *(A) Ability to process and handle confidential information with discretion.*
Week 6	Familiarizing with temporalities management	a. Evaluate parish facilities, maintenance, and repairs. b. Appreciate Safety and Security concerns c. Assess the technology infrastructure of the parish. d. Review contracted vs. organic services for the parish. e. Appraise the Parish Master Plan and capital campaign dynamics. *M6 Discussion Assignment:* *Conduct a physical survey of the parish facilities. You may want to have an informal conversation with the facilities supervisor, a designated maintenance employee, or informed parishioners. Describe parish facilities' general conditions and relate what you see as either potential or most needed improvements relative to the parish budget. In other words, how well are the facility needs*

| | | *addressed in the parish budget, and how well do they support present and future parish life needs? Summarize your impressions in 3-5 paragraphs and comment on at least two other postings (50 pts).*

(Note: If you would like the additional practice, its acceptable if your responses to other students are in Spanish)

Lleve a cabo una inspección de las facilidades físicas de la parroquia. Se sugiere tener una conversación informal con el supervisor de mantenimiento, un empleado de mantenimiento, o algún miembro de la parroquia al tanto de los detalles de la planta física de la parroquia. Describa las condiciones generales de las facilidades y asocia tus observaciones con lo que está programado en el presupuesto. En otras palabras, ¿están las prioridades actuales y futuras de planta física debidamente contemplados en el presupuesto? Resume tus impresiones en 3-5 párrafos y ofrece comentarios en las contestaciones de al menos dos otros estudiantes (50 puntos).

Topic 6: Knowledge, Skills, and Abilities (KSA)

(K) Knowledge of a wide range of temporalities maintenance and repair requirements.
(S) Skill in managing contingencies involving maintenance and repairs.
(A) Ability to assess site maintenance and repair needs and develop plans to address identified issues.
(K) Knowledge of applicable safety requirements for employees and parishioners on site. |

Week 7	Managing stewardship and development programs	a. Familiarize with Stewardship Programs as a means for community spiritual growth and its relation to parish administration. b. Evaluate risks of overemphasis on money and the need to emphasize the spiritual components of Stewardship to parish and staff. c. Assess and compare success cases in other dioceses to emphasize the value of stewardship to parish operations. d. Reflect on potential conflicts stemming from cultural understandings of stewardship within the parish and discuss the sensitivities needed as an administrator. *M7 Discussion Assignment:* *Search the web for what you think is a successful case of parish stewardship in the United States (web search). Compare and contrast the case you found with the stewardship efforts currently available in the parish of your current assignment. Take the viewpoint of the Administrator in your analysis. Consider the differences or similarities in demographics, resources, needs, and expectations for parish life development and present what you believe are opportunities for the parish of your current assignment. Summarize your suggestions and observations in 3-5 paragraphs and comment on at least two other postings (50 pts).* *(Note: If you would like the additional practice, its acceptable if your responses to other students are in Spanish)*

		Busque en la web un caso exitoso de "parish stewardship" en los Estados Unidos. Establezca una comparación entre el caso exitoso y los esfuerzos de "stewardship" (corresponsabilidad) en su parroquia asignada. Enfoque su análisis en torno a las funciones como Administrador. Considere las diferencias y semejanzas en características demográficas, recursos, necesidades, y expectativas para el crecimiento de su parroquia, y sugiera oportunidades que conduzcan a mejorías en su parroquia. Resume tus sugerencias en 3-5 párrafos y ofrece comentarios en las contestaciones de al menos dos otros estudiantes (50 puntos).
		Topic 7: Knowledge, Skills, and Abilities (KSA)
		(K) Knowledge of stewardship program objectives and requirements. (S) Skill in analyzing complex information and extract relevant conclusions.
		(S) Skill in identifying stewardship obstacles and develop options and implement solutions.
		(A) Ability to promote stewardship values in a multicultural environment.
Week 8	Interfacing with Diocesan functions and Programs and Skills Development	a. Relate to Diocesan Offices & Councils and the rationale for their functions and objectives. b. Appreciate diocesan programs that strengthen and protect parish life (e.g., Safe Environment, Catechist training)

		c. Review the primary roles of diocesan supporting agencies (Human Resources, Finance, Construction, Schools, Outreach, Healthcare, Retreat Centers). d. Become familiar with civil and canonical legal issues that affect the parish. *M8 Discussion Assignment:* *A majority of diocesan departmental and program leaders are hired because of their exceptional management skills reflecting more of a "corporate style" typical of a business executive rather than a "community-style" of communications more characteristic of an administrator or pastor. Granted, the parish business manager may feel more at ease in this environment. However, the significant decisions and implementation effectiveness of diocesan-driven activities still rely on the administrator or pastor. In what ways can one prepare for this potential conflict of communications styles? Offer how you would prepare for such a situation in 3-5 paragraphs, and remember to respond or comment to at least two other postings (50 pts).* *La mayoría de los líderes de programas y departamentos diocesanos son contratados debido a sus excepcionales habilidades de gestión que reflejan más un "estilo corporativo" típico de un ejecutivo de negocios que un "estilo comunitario" de comunicaciones más característico de un administrador o pastor. Por supuesto, el gerente de negocios de la parroquia puede sentirse más a gusto en este entorno, pero las decisiones importantes*

		y la efectividad de la implementación de las actividades impulsadas por la diócesis aún dependen del administrador o del párroco. ¿De qué manera se puede preparar uno para este posible conflicto de estilos de comunicación? Ofrezca cómo se prepararía para tal situación en 3-5 párrafos y recuerde responder o comentar al menos otras dos publicaciones (50 puntos). *Topic 8: Knowledge, Skills, and Abilities (KSA)* (K) Knowledge of diocesan resources and offices that support staff operations and parish life. (S) Skill in negotiation and facilitation. (A) Ability to analyze, organize and prioritize work while meeting multiple deadlines. (A) Ability to prepare documents, reports, and correspondence. (A) Ability to work effectively within a complex organizational structure.
Week 9	Developing administrative leadership and parish ministry (Ch 2)	a. Appreciate the relevance of ministry leadership formation concerning pastoral administration roles. b. Understand the basics of Volunteer Management as a component of parish life and staff support. c. Assess the value of new ministry opportunities and additional parish outreach programs and their impact on pastoral administration.

M9 Discussion Assignment:

Conduct an informal search by talking to a few ministry leaders and present what you found as the top 5 needs for ministry leader formation in your parish. Once ordained, explain your potential role in the development of ministry leaders along with the discoveries you have made in the current parish of your assignment. Relate the relevance of these needs to the administrator function. Summarize your impressions in 3-5 paragraphs and comment on at least two other postings (50 pts).

(Note: If you would like the additional practice, its acceptable if your responses to other students are in Spanish)

Lleve a cabo una investigación informal y determine cuales son las cinco (5) necesidades más urgentes en la formación de los dirigentes de ministerio en su parroquia asignada. Una vez ordenado, explique su rol en la formación de dirigentes ministeriales laicos en relación con los resultados de su investigación. Resume tus impresiones en 3-5 párrafos y ofrece comentarios en las contestaciones de al menos dos otros estudiantes (50 puntos)

Topic 9: Knowledge, Skills, and Abilities (KSA)

(K) Knowledge of ministry leadership skills within the pastoral setting.
(S) Skill in managing, motivating, and appreciating volunteer contributions to parish life.

		(S) Skill in forming leaders capable of effectively aligning their ministry activities with the overall goals and objectives of the parish. *(A) Ability to create awareness of the differences between secular and pastoral leadership dynamics.*
Week 10	Managing in a multicultural parish	a. Evaluate the need to educate staff for cultural sensitivity in the pastoral context. b. Recognize the relevance of pastoral language and cultural integration in parish operations. c. Appraise the value of planning and conducting integrational activities between staff and parish entities. c. Analyze your role as administrator in managing conflict among cultures within the parish setting. *M10 Discussion Assignment:* *Describe the effects of the Hispanic population in your assigned parish. Present your understanding of "flags" and "markers" you would use to assess progress towards a more integrated parish. How would you foster sensitivity in ministry leaders? What kind of experiential training would be best for you in learning how to become more pastorally sensitive to cultural differences? Summarize your comments and observations in 3-5 paragraphs and comment on at least two other postings (50 pts).* *(Note: If you would like the additional practice, its acceptable if your responses to other students are in Spanish)*

		Describa los efectos de la población Hispana en su parroquia. Determine qué tipo de tendencias positivas y negativas usarías como estrategia para crear una parroquia multicultural más integrada. ¿Cómo fomentarías más sensibilidad cultural entre los dirigentes ministeriales? ¿Qué clase de adiestramientos son más adecuados para cultivar en ti una mayor sensibilidad pastoral? Resume tus comentarios en 3-5 párrafos y ofrece comentarios en las contestaciones de al menos dos otros estudiantes (50 puntos). *Topic 10: Knowledge, Skills, and Abilities (KSA)* *(K) Knowledge of cultural dimension models and their relevance to conducting liturgies, religious formation, ministry group interactions, and social events.* *(S) Skill in managing tensions among cultural entities represented in the ministry* *(A) Ability to maintain a sense of true community in a multicultural parish.*
Week 11	Administering communications and information sharing	a. Review the effectiveness of traditional parish communications media. b. Discuss the relevance of integration and strategy for parish communications. c. Appreciate the significance of measuring the effectiveness of communications. d. Evaluate the viability of established contingency communications in the parish. e. Understand issues in dealing with public media.

<u>*M11 Discussion Assignment:*</u>

The sharing of information is essential to both community development (parish life) and parish organization (business operations). This means parishioners are exposed to both forms of communication. What seems to be the most effective community ways and business ways to share information with parishioners, and what areas of each do you believe need improvement or just do not work well? Summarize your impressions in 3-5 paragraphs and comment on at least two other postings (50 pts).

(Note: If you would like the additional practice, its acceptable if your responses to other students are in Spanish)

La distribución de información es esencial tanto para el desarrollo de la vida comunitaria (vida parroquial) como para las operaciones comerciales de la parroquia. A consecuencia, los miembros de la parroquia están expuestos a ambas formas de comunicación. ¿Cuáles les parece son las mejores formas de comunicar información a los fieles? ¿Qué parece ser efectivo y qué parece ser inefectivo? Resume tus observaciones en 3-5 párrafos y ofrece comentarios en las contestaciones de al menos dos otros estudiantes (50 puntos).

<u>*Topic 11: Knowledge, Skills, and Abilities (KSA)*</u>

(K) Knowledge of the role effective communication plays with respect to parish performance and functionality.

		(s) Skill in communicating orally and in writing to individuals, groups, and the public in a concise, clear, and well-supported manner using formats and technologies relevant to parish life. *(S) Skill in effectively and adequately respond to public relations issues.* *(A) Ability to evaluate communications strategies and select a strategy that leads to effective sharing of information, decision-making, and problem-solving.*
Week 12	Growing into the Administrator (Pastor) role (KSA) (Ch 8)	a. Discuss the design and relevance of the Administrator KSA Inventory. b. Discuss the dynamics of the administrator life cycle and administration transitions. c. Present materials from Small Business Administration (SBA) as a supplemental source of further training. d. Determine levels of administrator competencies and areas of development when comparing individual scores to pastor scores. *Final Assignment, Part 1 (100 pts)* *Complete the KSA inventory and compare your scores to the pastor scores. Reflect on the various competency (KSA) levels discussed in class and write in a 3-5 paragraph narrative your overall KSA score and your general concerning the pastor scores and your own observations by topic. What do you believe are your overall proficiencies? What areas require a more focused development over the next few years? How would you achieve them? Write your Part 1, but do not send it until*

| | | you have also completed the Part 2 next week. Both parts should be sent to the instructor in a single email during the last day of the semester.

Complete el inventario de KSA y compare sus puntajes con los puntajes de los párrocos. Reflexione sobre los diversos niveles de competencia (KSA) discutidos en clase y escriba en una narración de 3-5 párrafos su puntaje general KSA y su puntaje general en relación con los puntajes del pastor y sus propias observaciones por tema. ¿Cuáles cree que son sus competencias generales? ¿Qué áreas requieren un desarrollo más enfocado en los próximos años? ¿Cómo los conseguirías? Escriba su Parte 1, pero no la envíe hasta que también haya completado la Parte 2 la próxima semana. Ambas partes deben enviarse al instructor en un solo correo electrónico durante el último día del semestre.

<u>Topic 12: Knowledge, Skills, and Abilities (KSA)</u>

Use the Administrator KSA Inventory |
|---|---|---|
| Week 13 | Review, summary, and evaluation of course objectives | a. Discuss "Survey of Pastors" scores as a comparative baseline for personal scores and vocational growth planning. b. Discussion of the learning and value of this course. c. Suggested recommendations for the course. d. Suggested post-course activities as continuing maturation. |

		Final Course Assignment (Part 1 and Part 2): Over the past twelve modules, you explored and reflected on aspects of pastoral leadership and administration related to the pastor role. Through each module's live chats, discussions, and assignments, you delved into the broad landscape of parish life as a community and as an organization. What were the most significant discoveries or learning you derived from this course? In a 3-5 paragraph narrative, express the value this course had to your pastoral year experience. Send Part 1 and Part 2 (total of about 6-10 paragraphs) as a single email to the instructor. This assignment does not require any specific formatting or supporting sources since it is more a personal reflective than a scholarly submission.

PARTE 6 - OBJETIVOS Y METAS
ADMINISTRATIVAS

El Panorama de Aprendizaje Pastoral

PARTE 6

Administración de la parroquia

Este prontuario es una presentación estructurada de las funciones y responsabilidades de un administrador parroquial (párroco) en formato de curso académico. A continuación, se muestran los temas y objetivos de aprendizaje, las tareas sugeridas (en inglés y español), y los conocimientos, habilidades y habilidades (KSA) correspondientes a cada caso. El prontuario académico está configurado para un semestre de 13 semanas.

El prontuario también sirve de orientación, aunque no se disponga de un curso específico sobre administración de parroquias. Al alinearse con el objetivo de este manual, esta parte ofrece una visión integral de las responsabilidades administrativas con la intención de proporcionar una exposición inicial a los temas que de otra manera podrían faltar durante una experiencia más avanzada de la vida de la parroquia. Muchos de estos temas, especialmente los relacionados con las operaciones parroquiales, como Recursos Humanos, Finanzas, Temporalidades y Administración, toman tiempo para absorberlos. Sin embargo, poder familiarizarse con estos temas permite al seminarista la oportunidad de crecer en estos aspectos de la vida parroquial y moderar un poco el "trauma" de tener que pasar por un "curso intensivo sobre cómo convertirse en administrador años después en su vocación.

Este prontuario sugiere conferencias temáticas, estudios de casos, oradores invitados, discusión de estudiantes y autoevaluaciones para preparar al seminarista para el papel de liderazgo de la parroquia en lo que se refiere a la gestión y administración adecuada y efectiva de una parroquia. Este curso sugerido explora los problemas críticos que los párrocos y administradores típicamente enfrentarán. Los seminaristas examinarán diversas formas de abordar las técnicas eficaces de gestión y solución de problemas. El curso emplea un enfoque práctico que busca ayudar al seminarista a comprender el papel del Administrador-Pastor y cómo se relaciona con sus otras responsabilidades asociadas a la vida parroquial. La variedad de encargos presentados durante el curso tienen por objeto exponer al seminarista a una apreciación más profunda de la vida parroquial. También ayudará al seminarista a pensar estratégicamente.

OBJETIVOS	METAS
1. Fundaciones del liderazgo y la administración pastoral.	a. Concienciación sobre la influencia de los modelos de liderazgo y gestión de origen secular en la vida parroquial y la administración parroquial. b. El arraigo de los roles de liderazgo administrativo como otro paso a medida que la vocación evoluciona (identidad como clérigo). c. Revisar los modelos de administración-liderazgo secular y entender el Liderazgo Pastoral como una práctica espiritual.
2. Administrar a la parroquia como comunidad religiosa	a. Comprender la parroquia como *comunidad de fe* y revisar los roles del consejo pastoral parroquial como fundamento de la administración pastoral. b. Evaluar la vida parroquial usando indicadores de vitalidad parroquial y comprender su importancia con relación a las operaciones administrativas. c. Discutir la relevancia de la administración en la protección y orientación de la vida parroquial (crecimiento, transiciones, fusiones, cierres y sanación de traumas)
3. Evaluación de carismas parroquiales y visión comunitaria	a. Comprender los artefactos sociales para un proceso de concisión de la comunidad como marco para la administración pastoral. b. Diferenciar la planificación estratégica institucional y el papel del personal en el discernimiento estratégico parroquial. c. Reconocer diversos artefactos organizativos para conducir la vida comunitaria y su relación con el personal administrativo.

4. Control y contabilidad de los recursos financieros	a. Comprender los fundamentos de la contabilidad de los recursos financieros mediante la formulación de presupuestos y la presentación de informes financieros. b. Vea el valor de mantener fuentes de ingresos más allá de las recaudaciones dominicales. c. Agradece la pertinencia y las funciones del Consejo Financiero.
5. Comprender las operaciones de la parroquia	a. Apreciar las funciones y la dinámica de las operaciones del personal administrativo en relación con la vida parroquial. b. Resumir las funciones de Recursos Humanos y su rol en la administración. c. Comprender las funciones de empresas y agencias de apoyo externas a la parroquia. d. Revisar los sistemas de información parroquial. e. Familiarizarse con el mantenimiento de registros sacramentales.
6. Familiarizarse con la gestión de temporalidades	a. Evaluar el mantenimiento y las reparaciones de las instalaciones parroquiales. b. Apreciar las gestiones de seguridad. c. Evaluar la infraestructura tecnológica de la parroquia. d. Revisión de servicios contratados en contraste con los servicios internos de la parroquia. e. Revisar el Plan Maestro Parroquial y los temas de las campañas de capital para la construcción.
7. Gestión de programas de administración y desarrollo (Stewardship)	a. Familiarizarse con Programas de Administración (Stewardship) como medio para el crecimiento espiritual comunitario y su relación con la administración parroquial. b. Evaluar los riesgos de insistir demasiado en el dinero y la necesidad de hacer hincapié en los componentes espirituales de la Administración para parroquial y el personal.

c. Evaluar y comparar casos de éxito en otras diócesis para enfatizar el valor de la administración.

d. Reflexionar sobre los posibles conflictos derivados de entendimientos culturales de la administración dentro de la parroquia.

8. Interacción con funciones y programas diocesanas	a. Relacionar con las Oficinas y Consejos Diocesanos y la justificación de sus funciones y objetivos. b. Apreciar los programas diocesanos que fortalecen y protegen la vida parroquial (por ejemplo, entorno seguro, formación catequista) c. Examinar las principales funciones de los organismos de apoyo diocesanos (Recursos Humanos, Finanzas, Construcción, Escuelas, Promociones, Salud, Centros de Retirada). d. Familiarización con los aspectos legales-civiles y canónicos que afectan la parroquia.
9. Desarrollo del liderazgo administrativo y el ministerio de parroquia.	a. Apreciar la importancia de la formación de dirigentes ministeriales en relación con las funciones de administración pastoral. b. Comprender los aspectos básicos de la gestión de los voluntarios como componente de la vida parroquial y del apoyo al personal. c. Evaluar el valor de las nuevas oportunidades de los ministerios y de los nuevos programas de divulgación parroquial y sus repercusiones en la administración pastoral.
10. Gestión en una parroquia multicultural	a. Evaluar la necesidad de educar al personal para la sensibilidad cultural en el contexto pastoral. b. Reconocer la relevancia del lenguaje pastoral y la integración cultural en las operaciones parroquiales. c. Valorar la planificación y realización de actividades de integración cultural entre el personal y las entidades parroquiales. c. Analizar el rol como administrador en la gestión de conflictos entre culturas dentro de la vida parroquial.

11. Administración de comunicaciones e intercambio de información	a. Revisar la eficacia de los medios de comunicación parroquiales. b. Examinar la integración y la estrategia de los medios de comunicaciones parroquiales. c. Valorar la importancia de medir la eficacia de los medios. d. Evaluar la capacidad de las comunicaciones para manear una variedad de contingencias. e. Comprender los problemas al tratar con los medios de comunicaciones públicas.
12. Maduración de la vocación sacerdotal hacia el rol de administrador (párroco).	a. Analizar el diseño y la pertinencia del Inventario de KSA del Administrador. b. Discutir la dinámica del ciclo de vida del administrador y las transiciones de administración. c. Presentar materiales de la Administración de Pequeñas Empresas (SBA) como fuente complementaria de formación adicional. d. Determinar los niveles de competencia de los administradores y las áreas de desarrollo cuando se comparan las puntuaciones individuales con las puntuaciones de pastores.

PART 7 - ADMINISTRATOR'S KSA PROFILE

The Landscape of Pastoral Learning

PART 7

The Administrators KSA Profile©

Identifying and training for a proper level of parish administrative proficiency during seminary formation is a complex balancing act of expectations. On the one hand—because of a decreasing number of priests—some dioceses need parish administrators as soon as only a few years after ordination and expect performance levels somewhat comparable to experienced administrators or pastors. Consequently, there is pressure for more administrative courses, workshops, and webinars, preparing them for almost immediate assignments as administrators. On the other hand, seminarians desire to live out the first years of their priesthood, free of distracting activities, such as administration. The seminary is willing to accommodate some forms of administrative skills training, but only up to the point where these activities collide with its primary objectives of priestly formation. The business world has plenty of skill development programs available to satisfy diocesan and seminary expectations and is eager to assist. Add to this competing landscape of views that each diocese and parish is unique, which most likely also demands unique skills. All constituents would agree that administrative skills are necessary but disagree with when to train and to what degree. And even if the newly ordained becomes an effective manager, there is still the issue of becoming an effective leader.

One way to move forward within this complex environment is to assess the administrative proficiencies of each seminarian. Recognizing their strengths and insufficiencies allows him to target them as he moves forward in the maturation of his vocation and reminds him of the administrative duties commensurate with service as a Shepherd. This approach led to the development of the Parish Administration KSA Profile©.

The KSA Profile© was developed as an instrument to allow seminarians to compare their knowledge, skills, and abilities with those of a small sample of pastors. There are twelve topics of parish administration discussed weekly during a semester course. The complete list of topics and learning objectives were presented in Part 5 of this handbook, "Administration in Parish Life." These topics are presented again in Table 5.

A series of essential Knowledge, Skills, and Abilities (KSAs) were determined for each topic. Knowledge addresses the subject matter, topics, and items of information that a parish administrator should know for that topic. Knowledge represents <u>bodies of information</u> that are relevant to the performance of parish administration functions. Skills refer to technical or manual proficiencies, which are usually <u>learned or acquired through training</u>. Skills should be measurable and observable. Abilities address demonstrable capacities to apply several knowledge and skills simultaneously in order to complete a task. Abilities may also relate to personal and social attributes, which tend to be <u>innate or acquired without formal instructions</u>.

To illustrate how KSAs were determined, consider Topic 4 "Controlling and accounting of financial resources." The "Knowledge (K)" component of this topic is understanding accounting, budgetary, and parish financial practices and procedures. The

Table 5. Parish Administration Topics

Week	Course on Parish Administration
1	Foundations of Pastoral Leadership and Administration (Ch1,2)
2	Administering to the parish as a Faith Community (Ch 6)
3	Evaluating parish charisms and faith-vision (Ch 7)
4	Controlling and accounting of financial resources
5	Understanding parish business operations
6	Familiarizing with temporalities management
7	Managing stewardship and development programs
8	Interfacing with Diocesan functions and Programs
9	Developing administrative leadership and parish ministry (Ch 2)
10	Managing in a multicultural parish
11	Administering communications and information sharing
12	Growing into the Administrator (Pastor) role

"Skills(S)" component is being able to compose and analyze budgets and financial

statements. The "Ability (A)" part points to being able to manage a budget and work within the constraints of that budget. The same procedure was applied to each course topic, thereby identifying twelve knowledge areas, fifteen skills, and thirteen abilities. A Likert scale was created for each of these items, which as a whole make up the three sections of the KSA Profile (Knowledge, Skills, and Abilities) and a section at the end of the instrument to record the scores. The syllabus for the Parish Administration course presented in Part 5 lists the knowledge, skills, and abilities by topic.

As an example of how to use the instrument, Figure 1 provides the KSA scores of four seminarians. The first level of analysis is determining the highest and lowest scores for each KSA. For example, Seminarian A has low scores in K6 (*Knowledge of a wide range of temporalities maintenance and repair requirements*) and S5 (*Skill in composing budgets and reviewing financial statements*). Yet Seminarian B shows acceptable scores across all KSA's with the lowest score on K7 (*Knowledge of applicable safety requirements for employees and parishioners on-site*). Seminarian C has a low score on item A9 (*Ability to prepare documents, reports, and correspondence*), and Seminarian D shows low scores in two Knowledge and two Skill areas. The second level of analysis allows the seminarian to compare overall scores with a small sample of pastors. This second level of analysis includes the Pastor's high and low scored items.

Seminarian A

Knowledge		Skills		Abilities	
		S1	2		
		S2	2		
		S3	2	A1	2
K1	0	S4	2	A2	2
K2	2	S5	1	A3	2
K3	2	S6	3	A4	2
K4	2	S7	2	A5	2
K5	2	S8	2	A6	3
K6	1	S9	2	A7	2
K7	2	S10	2	A8	3
K8	2	S11	3	A9	2
K9	2	S12	2	A10	2
K10	3	S13	2	A11	2
K11	2	S14	3	A12	2
K12	3	S15	2	A13	2
Total	23	Total	32	Total	28

Seminarian B

Knowledge		Skills		Abilities	
		S1	3		
		S2	3		
		S3	3	A1	2
K1	2	S4	3	A2	2
K2	3	S5	3	A3	3
K3	3	S6	4	A4	2
K4	2	S7	3	A5	3
K5	2	S8	3	A6	3
K6	2	S9	3	A7	2
K7	1	S10	2	A8	3
K8	2	S11	3	A9	4
K9	2	S12	2	A10	4
K10	2	S13	3	A11	3
K11	2	S14	4	A12	2
K12	3	S15	3	A13	2
Total	26	Total	45	Total	35

Seminarian C

Knowledge		Skills		Abilities	
		S1	3		
		S2	3		
		S3	3	A1	3
K1	3	S4	3	A2	2
K2	3	S5	3	A3	3
K3	3	S6	3	A4	3
K4	3	S7	3	A5	3
K5	3	S8	3	A6	3
K6	1	S9	3	A7	3
K7	3	S10	3	A8	2
K8	3	S11	3	A9	3
K9	3	S12	3	A10	3
K10	3	S13	3	A11	3
K11	3	S14	3	A12	3
K12	3	S15	3	A13	3
Total	28	Total	37	Total	39

Seminarian D

Knowledge		Skills		Abilities	
		S1	3		
		S2	3		
		S3	3	A1	2
K1	1	S4	2	A2	2
K2	2	S5	2	A3	3
K3	1	S6	3	A4	4
K4	2	S7	3	A5	3
K5	2	S8	1	A6	3
K6	2	S9	1	A7	2
K7	2	S10	2	A8	3
K8	3	S11	3	A9	4
K9	3	S12	1	A10	3
K10	2	S13	2	A11	3
K11	2	S14	3	A12	2
K12	3	S15	2	A13	2
Total	28	Total	36	Total	38

Figure 1. Sample seminarian KSA scores

So far, 117 seminarians from more than 12 different dioceses over a six-year period have completed the Parish Administration KSA Profile© during their Pastoral Year, a 12-month internship where they are somewhat "free" from academics and living and ministering full-time within a parish. In analyzing these seminarian profiles, it is evident that administrative proficiencies are as varied as the diversity of personalities and previous experiences. A preliminary assumption was that assessments of Financial and Human Resources insufficiencies would be prevalent. And yet, a significant number of seminarians reported acceptable or better levels, especially among seminarians that had occupations before entering the seminary.

Hence, the approach suggested in this handbook is to assess the seminarian's administrative proficiency using the KSA Profile©. This approach allows the seminarian to (a) recognize his administrative strengths, (b) find opportunities to address the insufficiencies as he moves forward in the maturation of his vocation, and (c) be reminded of the administrative duties commensurate with service as a Shepherd. Therefore, upon an assignment as administrator, it would be a matter of reassessing the insufficiencies and learning the particularities of the diocese. This transition could occur either one-on-one with a mentor, employing skills-targeted workshops, or by other means. Nevertheless, it is worth remembering that even students with bachelor's degrees in Management are not immediately appointed managers, nor are graduate MBA students immediately selected as executives. In each of the cases, an experiential transition is warranted.

The pages that follow contain the full KSA© Profile and supporting materials. The profile on separate sheets is available upon request.

Pastoral Learning
Administration KSA Profile

The profile resulting from this assessment tool is intended to provide a representation of your current levels of knowledge, skills, and abilities required for Parish Administration. It reveals areas of strength and formation opportunities for administrative development as you mature in your administrative pastoral experiences.

Please respond to each of the statements below. Remember this is for your personal use in planning your development and as a tool to assist in formulating the last assignment of the Administrative Learning Objectives and Goals.

You can compare your scores with your current pastor or with those of seven experienced pastors located at the end of this assessment tool.

Knowledge Section(12): *This section addresses the subjects, topics, and information items that a parish administrator should know. Knowledge represents bodies of information that are relevant to the performance of parish administration functions.*

(K1) Knowledge of the fundamentals of secular leadership theory and most common models.

Poor	Passable	Good	Very Good	Excellent
0	1	2	3	4

(K2) Knowledge of the difference between "organization" and "community" as it applies to the parish setting.

Poor	Passable	Good	Very Good	Excellent
0	1	2	3	4

(K3) Knowledge of the difference between corporate strategic planning and parish strategic discerning.

Poor	Passable	Good	Very Good	Excellent
0	1	2	3	4

(K4) Knowledge of basic parish staff organizational functions and information systems.

Poor	Passable	Good	Very Good	Excellent
0	1	2	3	4

(K5) Knowledge of accounting, budgetary, and parish financial practices and procedures.

Poor	Passable	Good	Very Good	Excellent
0	1	2	3	4

(K6) Knowledge of a wide range of temporalities maintenance and repair requirements.

Poor	Passable	Good	Very Good	Excellent
0	1	2	3	4

(K7) Knowledge of applicable safety requirements for employees and parishioners on site.

Poor	Passable	Good	Very Good	Excellent
0	1	2	3	4

(K8) Knowledge of diocesan resources and offices that support staff operations and parish life.

Poor	Passable	Good	Very Good	Excellent
0	1	2	3	4

(K9) Knowledge of stewardship program objectives and requirements.

Poor	Passable	Good	Very Good	Excellent
0	1	2	3	4

(K10) Knowledge of leadership roles within the pastoral setting.

Poor	Passable	Good	Very Good	Excellent
0	1	2	3	4

(K11) Knowledge of cultural dimension models and their relevance to conducting liturgies, religious formation, ministry group interactions, and social events.

Poor	Passable	Good	Very Good	Excellent
0	1	2	3	4

(K12) Knowledge of the role effective communication plays concerning parish performance and functionality.

Poor	Passable	Good	Very Good	Excellent
0	1	2	3	4

Skills Section (15): This section addresses *technical or manual proficiencies, which are usually learned or acquired through training. Skills should be measurable and observable.*

(S1) Skill in rooting personal leadership practices from within the framework of a maturing priestly vocation.

Minimally Competent	Somewhat Competent	Competent	Very Competent	Highly Competent
0	1	2	3	4

(S2) Skill in adapting to change of parish assignment or pastors.

Minimally Competent	Somewhat Competent	Competent	Very Competent	Highly Competent
0	1	2	3	4

(S3) Skill in using social artifacts to inspire, unify and mobilize a parish community.

Minimally Competent	Somewhat Competent	Competent	Very Competent	Highly Competent
0	1	2	3	4

(S4) Skill in managing and supervising employees (full time & part time staff).

Minimally Competent	Somewhat Competent	Competent	Very Competent	Highly Competent
0	1	2	3	4

(S5) Skill in composing budgets and reviewing financial statements.

Minimally Competent	Somewhat Competent	Competent	Very Competent	Highly Competent
0	1	2	3	4

(S6) Skill in the use of standard office equipment and software.

Minimally Competent	Somewhat Competent	Competent	Very Competent	Highly Competent
0	1	2	3	4

(S7) Skill in managing contingencies involving maintenance and repairs.

Minimally Competent	Somewhat Competent	Competent	Very Competent	Highly Competent
0	1	2	3	4

(S8) Skill in negotiation and facilitation.

Minimally Competent	Somewhat Competent	Competent	Very Competent	Highly Competent
0	1	2	3	4

(S9) Skill in analyzing complex information and extract relevant conclusions.

Minimally Competent	Somewhat Competent	Competent	Very Competent	Highly Competent
0	1	2	3	4

(S10) Skill in identifying stewardship obstacles and develop options and implement solutions.

Minimally Competent	Somewhat Competent	Competent	Very Competent	Highly Competent
0	1	2	3	4

(S11) Skill in managing, motivating, and appreciating volunteer contributions to parish life.

Minimally Competent	Somewhat Competent	Competent	Very Competent	Highly Competent
0	1	2	3	4

(S12) Skill in forming leaders capable of effectively aligning their ministry activities with the overall goals and objectives of the parish.

Minimally Competent	Somewhat Competent	Competent	Very Competent	Highly Competent
0	1	2	3	4

(S13) Skill in managing tensions among cultural entities represented in ministry.

Minimally Competent	Somewhat Competent	Competent	Very Competent	Highly Competent
0	1	2	3	4

(S14) Skill in communicating orally and in writing to individuals, groups and the public in a concise, clear and well-supported manner using formats and technologies relevant to parish life.

Minimally Competent	Somewhat Competent	Competent	Very Competent	Highly Competent
0	1	2	3	4

(S15) Skill in effectively and properly respond to public relations issues.

Minimally Competent	Somewhat Competent	Competent	Very Competent	Highly Competent
0	1	2	3	4

Abilities Section (13): This section addresses *demonstrable capacities to apply several knowledge and skills to complete a task simultaneously. Abilities may also relate to personal and social attributes, which tend to be innate or acquired without formal instructions.*

(A1) Ability in recognizing secular model insufficiencies when applied to the parish environment.

Minimally Competent	Somewhat Competent	Competent	Very Competent	Highly Competent
0	1	2	3	4

(A2) Ability to recognize needs and growth patterns in parish life.

Minimally Competent	Somewhat Competent	Competent	Very Competent	Highly Competent
0	1	2	3	4

(A3) Ability to identify parish charisms and use them as a framework for pastoral work.

Minimally Competent	Somewhat Competent	Competent	Very Competent	Highly Competent
0	1	2	3	4

A4) Ability to work collaboratively and build positive relations with employees, peers, volunteers, and contractors.

Minimally Competent	Somewhat Competent	Competent	Very Competent	Highly Competent
0	1	2	3	4

(A5) Ability to process and handle confidential information with discretion.

Minimally Competent	Somewhat Competent	Competent	Very Competent	Highly Competent
0	1	2	3	4

(A6) Ability to manage a budget and work within the constraints of that budget.

Minimally Competent	Somewhat Competent	Competent	Very Competent	Highly Competent
0	1	2	3	4

(A7) Ability to assess site maintenance and repair needs and develop plans to address identified issues.

Minimally Competent	Somewhat Competent	Competent	Very Competent	Highly Competent
0	1	2	3	4

(A8) Ability to analyze, organize and prioritize work while meeting multiple deadlines.

Minimally Competent	Somewhat Competent	Competent	Very Competent	Highly Competent
0	1	2	3	4

(A9) Ability to prepare documents, reports, and correspondence.

Minimally Competent	Somewhat Competent	Competent	Very Competent	Highly Competent
0	1	2	3	4

(A10) Ability to work effectively within a complex organizational structure.

Minimally Competent	Somewhat Competent	Competent	Very Competent	Highly Competent
0	1	2	3	4

(A11) Ability to promote stewardship values in a multicultural environment.

Minimally Competent	Somewhat Competent	Competent	Very Competent	Highly Competent
0	1	2	3	4

(A12) Ability to create awareness of the differences between secular and pastoral leadership dynamics.

Minimally Competent 0	Somewhat Competent 1	Competent 2	Very Competent 3	Highly Competent 4

(A13) Ability to evaluate communications strategies and select a strategy that leads to effective sharing of information, decision-making, and problem solving.

Minimally Competent 0	Somewhat Competent 1	Competent 2	Very Competent 3	Highly Competent 4

End of assessment

Next, transcribe your values from each of the previous statements for Knowledge (K), Skills(S) and Abilities (A) into the table below and add them up by column.

Knowledge	Skills	Abilities
	S1	
	S2	
	S3	A1
K1	S4	A2
K2	S5	A3
K3	S6	A4
K4	S7	A5
K5	S8	A6
K6	S9	A7
K7	S10	A8
K8	S11	A9
K9	S12	A10
K10	S13	A11
K11	S14	A12
K12	S15	A13
Total K _____	Total S _____	Total A _____

KSA definitions

- **Knowledge** Section(12): *This section addresses the subjects, topics, and items of information that an parish administrator should know. Knowledge represents bodies of information that are relevant to the performance of parish administration functions.*
- **Skills** Section (15): This section addresses *technical or manual proficiencies which are usually learned or acquired through training. Skills should be measurable and observable.*
- **Abilitie**s Section (13): This section addresses *demonstrable capacities to apply several knowledge and skills simultaneously in order to complete a task. Abilities may also relate to personal and social attributes which tend to be innate or acquired without formal instructions.*

Either compare with your pastor (if he can complete a form) or compare with the seven experienced pastor scores below:

KNOWLEDGE SCORES, EXPERIENCED PASTORS

Use your <u>printed copy</u> of the inventory for KSA interpretations

	P1	P2	P3	P4	P5	P6	P7		
K1	2	0	1	0	2	3	3		LOW
K2	2	1	2	2	4	2	3		
K3	1	0	1	2	4	2	2		
K4	1	0	1	3	4	2	4		
K5	0	2	1	3	3	2	4		
K6	1	1	1	3	3	2	4		
K7	1	0	1	1	3	3	4		
K8	2	2	3	4	4	4	4		HIGH
K9	1	3	2	3	3	0	4		
K10	1	3	3	3	4	2	4		
K11	1	0	4	2	4	4	2		
K12	1	4	2	3	4	4	3		
TK	14	16	22	29	42	30	41	AVG K	28

Average Pastor Score for Knowledge= 28 pts

Lowest Score(s)

(K1) <u>Knowledge of the fundamentals of secular leadership theory and most common models.</u>

Poor	Passable	Good	Very Good	Excellent
0	1	2	3	4

Highest Score(s)

(K8) <u>Knowledge of diocesan resources and offices that support staff operations and parish life.</u>

Poor	Passable	Good	Very Good	Excellent
0	1	2	3	4

Ronald R. Rojas

SKILLS SCORES, EXPERIENCED PASTORS

	P1	P2	P3	P4	P5	P6	P7		
S1	1	2	2	3	4	3	4		High
S2	2	3	1	2	4	3	4		High
S3	1	0	2	0	3	2	2		
S4	0	4	1	2	4	1	4		Low
S5	0	3	0	3	3	3	4		
S6	0	2	2	2	3	3	3		
S7	1	0	1	2	3	3	2		
S8	0	4	1	3	4	2	2		
S9	0	2	1	2	3	2	1		
S10	1	1	1	3	3	0	4		
S11	1	3	2	2	3	4	4		High
S12	1	3	2	3	3	3	3		
S13	0	2	3	1	3	3	0		
S14	0	3	2	2	3	3	2		
S15	0	2	2	2	3	3	2		
TS	8	34	23	32	49	38	41	AVG-S	32

Average Score for Skills= 32 pts

Highest Score(s)

(S1) Skill in rooting personal leadership practices from within the framework maturing priestly vocation.

Minimally Competent	Somewhat Competent	Competent	Very Competent	Highly Competent
0	1	2	3	4

(S2) Skill in adapting to change of parish assignment or pastors.

Minimally Competent	Somewhat Competent	Competent	Very Competent	Highly Competent
0	1	2	3	4

(S11) Skill in managing, motivating and appreciating volunteer contributions to parish life.

Minimally Competent	Somewhat Competent	Competent	Very Competent	Highly Competent
0	1	2	3	4

Lowest Score(s)

(S4) Skill in managing and supervising employees (full time & part time staff).

Minimally Competent	Somewhat Competent	Competent	Very Competent	Highly Competent
0	1	2	3	4

ABILITY SCORES, EXPERIENCED PASTORS

	P1	P2	P3	P4	P5	P6	P7		
A1	1	0	3	0	3	1	3	Low	
A2	1	2	2	2	4	3	3		
A3	1	2	4	2	4	3	3	High	
A4	1	4	4	3	4	3	4		
A5	2	4	2	4	4	4	4		
A6	0	2	1	3	4	3	3		
A7	1	0	2	3	4	3	2		
A8	1	1	4	3	4	3	2		
A9	0	2	2	3	3	3	4		
A10	1	2	4	3	3	1	4		
A11	1	1	4	3	3	0	3		
A12	1	2	1	3	4	3	3		
A13	0	1	2	3	3	3	4		
TA	11	23	35	35	47	33	42	AVG-A	32

Average Score for Abilities= 32 pts

Highest Score(s)

(A3) **Ability to identify parish charisms and use them as a framework for pastoral work.**

Minimally Effective	Somewhat Effective	Effective	Very Effective	Highly Effective
0	1	2	3	4

Lowest Score(s)

(A1) **Ability in recognizing secular model insufficiencies when applied to the parish environment.**

Minimally Effective	Somewhat Effective	Effective	Very Effective	Highly Effective
0	1	2	3	4

PART 8 - PASTORAL LEADERSHIP

Developing pastoral leadership competencies

PART 8

Developing pastoral leadership competencies

In following the previous section on parish administration and in providing a landscape of objectives, this section addresses topics associated with the framing and development of pastoral leadership qualities. Just as Management and Leadership are recognized as different yet related academic disciplines, Parish Administration and Pastoral Leadership are treated in this handbook as distinct but interrelated subjects.

The ability to recognize valuable and unfavorable consequences of secularly derived leadership models is the most fundamental challenge of any leadership model applied to the pastoral setting. Since leadership concepts are socially constructed and culturally bound (Mellahi,2000), models built for the business, non-profit, government, military, or academic sectors are best suited for their respective industries. Although their availability may lure them into parish life, their indiscriminate use, particularly in sectors for which they were never intended, has already proven to be deeply problematic.

Evaluating the underlying assumptions of secular models and contrasting their definitional components with the proper understanding of the pastoral intent is essential to enacting effective leadership in the parish. As a starting point for this analysis, the academic disciplines typically present the advantages and disadvantages of leadership models in their course textbooks. For example, the Peter Northouse textbook on leadership (*Leadership Theory and Practice*: Sage, 2016) dedicates entire chapters and sections on the advantages and disadvantages of the most prevalent leadership models. To illustrate the relevance of carefully assessing leadership models, take a commonly used model in the Church setting, the Servant Leadership model. The advantages and disadvantages of Northouse (2016) are listed in Table 6.

Table 6. Example, Analysis of the Servant Leadership model

Advantages	Disadvantages
Altruism is the central component of the model.	Recognized more as a "Followership" model than a Leadership model.
Leaders do not dominate but should share control and influence.	Still debate among scholars as to what exactly are its core elements.
Research shows conditions where this model works and does not work.	Prescribes that "good leaders" put others above self.
Reliable and valid measurements of this model are available.	Unclear as to whether the model promotes a behavior or a concept.

Source: Northouse (2016) *Leadership: Theory and Practice*, Sage (pp.239-241)

Northhouse (2016) notes "altruism" as a main component of Servant Leadership, but also cautions it is truly a Followership model, not a Leadership model, and therefore influence and control is shared. Does a priest as Shepherd share control and influence with parishioners? He also states there are places where this model is effective and where it is not. Then what does the research say about using this model in the parish setting? The fact that scholars are still debating the core elements of this model implies a high degree of ambiguity and uncertainty in its application. Do these ambiguities present risks? More importantly, some research has already established that Servant Leadership is detrimental to the priesthood. In "Evolving visions of the priesthood," Hogue and Wenger (2003) make a significant finding:

> We have additional data from research on men who have already left the priesthood. Both in 1970 and in 2000, the men who had resigned from the priesthood told investigators that they held to a more servant-leader, participatory model of priesthood that the priests who have remained in service (p. 125)

Although the model is appealing, it does present risks and possible unintended consequences that require caution. A similar analysis on other models—such as transformational leadership, spiritual leadership, adaptive leadership, and situational leadership—may be warranted if they are intended to be promoted within a pastoral setting. A similar analysis is also advisable for leadership fads. Notably, none of these models address the essential component of formation as defined by the Church, a leadership model centered on God's grace.

Among the variety of leadership models available within the secular world and the leadership discipline are the traits, competencies, behavioral, situational, transformational, ethical, and cultural approaches. Although most of these models address elements of the Human and Intellectual dimensions in general, they lack aspects that are essential to the Pastoral and Spiritual dimensions of formation. Given that formation occurs along these four dimensions, it is reasonable to assume that any leadership modeling specifically oriented towards the parish setting would emerge and remain connected to all these dimensions. More importantly, it would also be rooted in the Church's definition of formation, that it remains rooted in cooperation with God's grace:

> Formation, as the Church understands it, is not equivalent to a secular sense of schooling or, even less, job training. Formation is first and foremost cooperation with the grace of God." (PPF5, n.68).

A competency-based approach is necessary to accommodate the dimensions of formation into a pastoral leadership model that, at the same time, is coherent with the evolution of the leadership discipline. This form of modeling stresses the importance of being conceptualized around formation, closer to what is expected from a pastor, is intuitively appealing, allows a broader view of Church, while remaining consistent with many other structures of leadership development. Of course, the breadth of possible skills can go beyond what may be needed as a leader, and its application is limited to the parish context. This means there are few training programs specifically designed to teach leadership modeling with this approach.

There are expected competencies crucial to the exercise of leadership

Ronald R. Rojas

for the pastoral setting yet lacking in the past and current secular models. Fundamental competencies for the pastoral setting include:

(a) Vocation (calling) awareness
(b) Character strength
(c) Relational competency
(d) Community (which is different from organizational competency)
(e) Discernment competency (inclusive of prayer, reflection, and contemplation)
(f) Pastoral awareness (love as a rationale for behavior and action)
(g) A "directing" competency, based upon the orchestration of activities revealed by Divine Providence rather than just by a leader's desires.

These competencies are also valuable criteria when assessing the value and limitations of secular models (or business models) being used in the pastoral setting. Again, suffice it to say that while secular models permeate ministry leadership by means of the laity, pastoral leadership as a competency model is a more desirable construct for the parish setting and merits recognition and promulgation. Furthermore, these competencies are conjoined to God's grace, a tenant of pastoral formation.

Just as the previous course syllabus, this syllabus is a structured presentation of pastoral leadership within the broader context of Church and the leadership discipline. The syllabus is also configured for a 13-week semester.

Course outlines for Pastoral Leadership Course

Date	Module	Goals and discussion topics
Week 1	1. The historical development of leadership and sector-specific leadership models.	a. Review the history and recent developments in leadership modeling as a contextual foundation to pastoral leadership. b. Discuss the issues related to sources of power and consider the latest definitions of leadership as influence. c. Developing an awareness of the influence of secularly generated leadership and management models in parish life and parish administration. d. Examine the most common models of secular leadership and contrast them with the current leadership programs in the Church.
Week 2	2. Comparing the concepts of "organization" and "community" and their value to the institutional life.	a. Discuss the definitions and implications of the "organization" and "community" constructs as described in the scholarly literature. b. Comprehend parish as *faith community* and review the opportunities and challenges of the pastoral council as a leadership organism. c. Review and analyze the quantitative and qualitative methods to assess pastoral effectiveness in parish life. d. Discuss the relevance of current trends in parish and schools/universities, especially in light of the "new normal" and post-pandemic era.

Week 3	3. The competencies of pastoral leadership as a spiritual practice.	a. Discuss the value of integrating the leadership competencies as an aspect of the personal discovery (vocation and personal identity) b. Consider the practical effects of character strength and character development for the leadership function. c. Recognize the implications of spiritual practices and spiritual growth as a component of leadership development. d. Evaluate discernment models and assess opportunities for developing discernment capacity in parish (institutional) life.
Week 4	4. Leadership and vision: Artifacts and models to provide direction, growth, and change in the parish setting.	a. Understand the basics of social artifacts envisioning processes as a pastoral leadership device. b. Differentiate between corporate strategic planning and the pastoral leader's role in practicing strategic discerning. c. Recognize various organizational artifacts to guide community life and its connection to ministry leadership and parish staff. d. Identify the leader's need for contingency planning (e.g., parish and school closings, mergers, pandemic) and discuss the prospects and constraints associated with parishes and schools' contingency planning.
Week 5	5. Preserving and fostering Catholic identity and culture in parishes, schools, universities, and non-profit organizations.	a. Review and discuss the relevance of institutional identity and culture in parishes, schools, universities, and non-profit organizations, b. Analyze the internal and external forces that sustain and weaken a Catholic institution's identity and culture.

		c. Discuss the relationship between leadership and culture within a Catholic organization. d. Delineate potential topics for further research related to leadership styles and institutional identity.
Week 6	6. Research, assessments, and development of programs for parish ministry leaders.	a. Appreciate the relevance of ministry leadership formation concerning pastoral competencies and effectiveness. b. Recognize the opportunities to tailor and adapt continued leadership development for ministry leaders within the parish setting. c. Review and synthesize reports and studies on the urgency and value of ministry leadership development. d. Discuss the basics of Volunteer Management as a component of Catholic institutional life and leadership development. e. Assess the value of new ministry opportunities and additional parish outreach programs and their impact on pastoral practice.
Week 7	7. Leadership challenges, models, and tensions of Evangelizing in a multicultural organization.	a. Evaluate the need to educate leaders for cultural sensitivity in the pastoral context. b. Recognize the relevance of pastoral language and cultural integration in parish operations. c. Appraise the value of planning and conducting integrational activities between staff and parish entities. c. Analyze your role in dealing with conflict among cultures within the parish setting.

Week 8	8. Leveraging the leadership function through effective forms of communication and learning.	a. Recognize the variety of communications skills and learning styles available to a pastoral leader. b. Review the effectiveness of different communications and learning media concerning parish demographics. c. Discuss the relevance of integration, consistency, and strategy in parish communications platforms. d. Evaluate the value of contingency communications and issues when dealing with public media.
Week 9	9. Recognize the relevance of networking with other communities (parishes, outreach programs, and diocesan functions).	a. Relate to Diocesan Offices & Councils and the rationale for their functions and objectives. b. Appreciate diocesan programs that strengthen and protect parish life (e.g., Safe Environment, Catechist training) c. Review the primary roles of diocesan supporting agencies (Human Resources, Finance, Construction, Schools, Outreach, Healthcare, Retreat Centers) d. Discuss the possible opportunities and tensions associated with developing networking capacity in parish and school (university) life.
Week 10	10. Understand a researcher's approach to design, implementation, and assessments of ministry practicums.	a. Appreciate the relevance of pastoral formation concerning the quality of pastoral care in parish life. b. Research and evaluate the validity and reliability of available Church leadership courses, ministry practicums, and pastoral learning programs.

		c. Review and analyze the range of knowledge (K), Skills (S), and abilities (A) expected of pastoral leaders. d. Assess levels of pastoral leadership competencies and areas of development. e. Discuss the dynamics and effects of the pastor (administrator) life-cycle and leadership transitions.
Week 11	11. Appreciate the value of models and practice of relational theory and pastoral imagining.	a. Recognize the fundamentals of relational theory across multiple disciplines and evaluate its relevance to pastoral leadership. b. Discuss the implications of the Hierarchy of Relationships to the leadership function. c, Analyze case studies in parish life of effective and ineffective applications of relations theory. d. Relate the discussions and learning to personal development.
Week 12	12. Recognize a secular view of pastoral leadership: Spiritual leadership and Spirituality in the workplace.	a. Review the historical development and current literature on Spirituality in the Workplace. b. Compare and contrast the secular (workplace) and Church understanding of spirituality and its relevance to pastoral leadership. c. Discuss the value and problems of assessing the spirituality construct. d. Evaluate opportunities and challenges in developing spiritual growth in small groups and communities.

Week 13	13. Discuss the future of secular and pastoral leadership and explore practical research opportunities for possible thesis development.	a. Discuss "Survey of Pastors" scores as a comparative baseline for personal scores and vocational growth planning. b. Exchange impressions on this course's learning and value with the overall curriculum and suggest potential research topics. c. Encourage submission of manuscripts to popular and scholarly publications on timely pastoral topics. d. Suggest post-course activities as continuing maturation efforts towards a more effective enactment of Ecclesial Leadership.

PART 9 - "TEACHING PARISH" CRITERIA

The Landscape of Pastoral Learning

PART 9

"Teaching Parish" Criteria

This last part of the handbook addresses a set of suggested criteria for a Teaching Parish. In many ways, the requirements mirror the structure and intent of Teaching Hospitals in establishing a learning environment. Here the components of the Teaching Parish are the pastor, the group that is responsible for assisting in the pastoral experiences processing, the seminarian, and of course, the seminary. The preferred name given to the laity group responsible for providing pastoral insights to the seminarian is "Vocation Mentoring Board" since it emphasizes and reminds members of its primary purpose, that of vocation mentoring. Other terms have been used, such as the Vocation Mentoring Team, Pastoral Teaching Committee, and others. But what matters is taking advantage of the laity's perspective for pastoral learning. Of course, the pastor can provide interpretations from his point of view. But allowing the learner a firsthand experience in receiving insights from the laity's point of view may validate or be different than the pastor's perspective, and therefore, adds value to the formation process. It is possible this lay group may not know much about priest formation from the seminary's point of view, but they are undoubtedly able to articulate what they want and expect from a priest.

Regarding the group responsible for assisting in the processing of the pastoral experience, three models are possible. One model is where the group members remain constant throughout the year and where the members assume the responsibility to go and observe the learners' experiences against the learning plan. A second model is where the chair (or president) is the only permanent member during the learning agreement period. For this model, representatives from the different ministries or parish activities the learner have selected are the ones that make up the group. In this case, the members can vary from year to year depending on the learner's selection of ministries and the learning agreement. Of course, a third possible model is a hybrid where some members are permanent, and others are invited as necessary.

What is said earlier in this handbook about the five conceptual underpinnings to improve the mindset that drives the pastoral learning environment in a parish setting is essential to this group. Again, (a) the significance of the term "vocation," (b) Church guidance for pastoral learning, (c) principles of experiential learning, (d) the difference between career mentoring and pastoral mentoring, and (e) the value of group processing of pastoral experiences, are all at the core of this group's effectiveness.

Naturally, these criteria can and should be modified to accommodate for the best learning environment possible. It is also necessary to recognize that not all parishes are "called" to be teaching parishes, just as not all hospitals are teaching hospitals. It's not only about meeting specific minimal criteria. A teaching parish provides exemplary ministry services and is serious about the formation throughout the many aspects of parish life. Of course, the pastor's willingness and desires are essential, but also the willingness and desires of parish ministries and staff to help shoulder the pastoral dimension of formation for seminarians (or of those in formation for the permanent diaconate) as well as their ability to help translate pastoral experiences into pastoral learning. The combination of knowledge, ministerial experience, the continuous efforts made throughout the parish to improve pastoral competencies, and parish vitality make a unique environment for pastoral learning.

Below are the five suggested criteria offered as a minimum to establish a Teaching Parish.

Criteria 1: *The pastor agrees to collaborate in the formation of seminarians into parish life experiences.*

1.1 The Pastor has informed Ministries, Staff, & Vocation Mentoring Board of the need and value of this program for the parish and the seminarian's pastoral development.

1.2 The learning objectives for each seminarian have been agreed upon with the Pastor and are feasible to accomplish within the realities of the parish setting.

1.3 The Pastor formally establishes a Vocation Mentoring Board.

1.4 The Pastor submits written evaluations to the Seminary, and the Office at the Seminary (typically, the Dean of Pastoral Formation) distributes them to the appropriate forums.

Criteria 2: *The Vocation Mentoring Board member demonstrates a willingness to mentor seminarians into parish life experiences.*

2.1 Vocation Mentoring Board members are sufficiently familiar with parish, church, and priestly formation.

2.2 Vocation Mentoring Board members agree to dedicate time and effort to mentor the seminarians and work closely with the pastor and the seminary formators.

2.3 Vocation Mentoring Board members offer an agreed-upon set of meaningful and insightful mentorship observations.

2.4 Vocation Mentoring Board members recognize that privacy and confidentiality are essential to the mentoring process and maintain a climate of positive, open dialogue with the seminarian.

Criteria 3: *Mentorship environment for the pastoral development of seminarians.*

3.1 The Vocation Mentoring Board provides insights to the seminarians at least two times every semester, preferably mid-semester and at the end of the semester. In rare cases, written observations may be required.

3.2 The Vocation Mentoring Board ensures seminarians are mentored primarily in the types of parish activities that best match the learning objectives selected for the observation period.

3.3 The Vocation Mentoring Board has sufficient interactions with the parish activities corresponding to the seminarian's learning objectives so they can offer meaningful insights during the mentoring sessions.

3.4 The Vocation Mentoring Board members have attended the mentorship familiarization seminar or workshop offered by the seminary.

Criteria 4: *Seminary actions related to the Parish Learning program.*

4.1 Seminarians receive reimbursement by the seminary for mileage and tolls incurred during travel to the parish.

4.2 Seminarians will be aware of the learning objectives before engaging in parish activities.

4.3 The seminary will conduct program training for the Vocation Mentoring Board (e.g., mentorship workshop) and periodically conduct follow-up visits.

Criteria 5: *Seminarian actions related to the Parish Learning experience*

5.1 Seminarians review the Landscape of Pastoral Objectives and Goals (handbook) and the inputs provided by the pastors on available ministries at the Teaching Parish and finalize a Learning Agreement.

5.2 As a general rule, it is anticipated the seminarians would discern for not more than 5 areas from the Landscape of Pastoral objectives (handbook).

5.3 Seminarians receive verbal observations from the Vocation Mentoring Board.

5.4 At the end of the session, each participating seminarian composes and submits a reflective paper on the most significant learning events and challenges, a summary of Vocation Mentoring Board observations, as well as suggestions for the next pastoral experience.

5.5 This reflective is submitted to the course instructor before the end of the semester.

5.6 The seminary dean of pastoral formation distributes them to the appropriate seminary forums.

PART 10 - EVALUATIONS AND ASSESSMENTS

The Landscape of Pastoral Learning

PART 10

Evaluations and Assessments

Evaluations and assessments of pastoral learning are necessary to ensure the best possible processes, learn from shortcomings, consider modifications, and judge the short and long-term outcomes. Accordingly, evaluation of the learner's performance against the learning plan, a parish appraisal, and a program assessment are key activities directed at a continuous improvement effort. Below is a discussion related to each of these three areas of assessment.

A. Learner Evaluation

The context for a pastoral learner's evaluation is the Learning Agreement. The samples on the next page provide an example of a Learning Agreement and a suggested evaluation form (Figures 2 and 3). The evaluation form is a combination of quantitative and qualitative observations. The quantitative assessment is a simple 0-3 scale (0 = No progress to 3 = Significant progress), where the learner provides an "impression" of objective and goal accomplishments for each category (Vocation Development, Ministry Engagement, Judgment and Decision-making, and Pastoral Awareness). The form also provides space for qualitative comments and observations that support the numeric assessment and an area on the back of the form for additional comments. The distribution of the evaluation form is up to the Dean of Pastoral Formation.

For those following the parish administration or the pastoral leadership syllabus, the course itself is the learning agreement, and each course has its own end-of-semester evaluation instrument. Indeed, all assessment instruments mentioned in this handbook can be modified to accommodate evaluations of pastoral learning for men in formation for the permanent diaconate as well as for lay learners.

B. Parish Evaluation

The most prevalent practice for a parish assessment of a pastoral learner's outcomes is the pastor's evaluation, and the form used is typically an email or a letter. The assessment of a pastor's mentoring effectiveness and degree of engagement in the program is typically conducted by the Dean of Pastoral Formation.

The Vocation Mentoring Board offers verbal insights directly to the seminarian during their sessions but does not provide any written evaluation to the seminary. Significant observations by the board can be forwarded to the pastor (if the pastor cannot attend the sessions) to be included in the pastor's evaluation.

However, it is recommended that the board conduct its own internal performance assessment using the criteria outlined within the instructions section presented at the beginning of this handbook. Appropriate considerations are, for example, *"How well did our insights delate to vocation, Church guidance, experiential learning, pastoral mentoring, and our processing of pastoral experiences?"* This evaluation mode (dialogue) is less structured but relevant to maintaining and improving a proper learning environment. A list of statements and promptings is offered in Table 7 as a way to assess the verbal interactions with the learner. Indeed, the board can also benefit from the pastor's remarks on its performance.

The Vocation Mentoring Board may also want to assess the effectiveness either by itself or by means of a facilitator. In a case where there are a large number of parishes in a teaching parish program, it is recommended to train and make available a team of facilitators to ensure the boards are operating according to Teaching Parish expectations and act as an independent resource for evaluating board performance. A complete list of facilitator functions is presented in Table 8. As a result of its evaluation, the board may decide to change members or consider a different model based on its past evaluation cycle experiences. There are three possible models for board functioning, and selecting the most suitable model may be a function of how the board interprets its abilities to provide meaningful insights and the learner's plans (Figure 3). Model 1 is where the board members are permanently assigned and are tasked to either attend the same settings as the learner or seek inputs from the ministry participants.

Sample Learning Agreement

Name: _____

Cohort: 2d Year Theology

Teaching Parish: St. Paul

Please, describe your Pastoral Learning Objectives
  OBJECTIVES-GOALS RELATED TO VOCATION DEVELOPMENT
  6. Recognize how personal attitudes, values, and prejudices affect pastoral ministry (H, P).
      b. Demonstrate the ability to identify and manage personal biases that may limit pastoral
      effectiveness.

  OBJECTIVES-GOALS RELATED TO MINISTRY ENGAGEMENT
  8. Recognize the developmental value of actively engaging in community dynamics.
      b. Demonstrate the ability to recognize and engage in learning opportunities prompted by
      interpersonal tensions within a small community or group setting.

  OBJECTIVES-GOALS RELATED TO JUDGEMENT & DECISION-MAKING
  20. Recognize situations where the ministry of presence is the most valuable pastoral response (H, S, P).
      a. Demonstrate initiative in finding opportunities to be available to others and respond with
      pastoral presence.

  OBJECTIVES-GOALS RELATED TO PASTORAL AWARENESS
  32. Recognize and value the contribution of women to church leadership and parish life (H, I, P).
      c. Demonstrate the ability to foster the contributions and gifts of women in parish life.

Please, indicate the ministries which you and your pastor agreed upon for this year (Describe the specific times
and days for your selected ministries):
  Ministry of Presence — presence before, during, and after Sunday Masses
  Adult Faith Formation, Adult Spiritual Enrichment.
  RCIA, marriage preparation classes, or/and baptismal preparation classes.
  Attending Parish Functions
  RCIA - TBA Starts October 18
  ALPHA / Adult Faith Formation, Thursday 7pm - 8:30pm
  Social Media - 3x a week on Facebook and Instagram
  Mass Streaming Engagement - Sunday 10am Mass

☐ I confirm that my pastor agrees to these choices and has received a copy of this Agreement.

☐ I confirm that my Formation Advisor agrees to these choices and received a copy of this Agreement.

☐ I confirm that the Chair of the Vocation Mentoring Board has received a copy of this Agreement.

Learner Initials: _____

Date completed: _____

Figure 2. Sample Learning Agreement

Name: **Formator:**

Period: Date submitted

Learner Initials: Meeting Date:

Assessment of Objectives and goals for this period	0. No progress 2, Satisfactory progress 1. Minimal progress 3. Significant progress
VOCATION DEVELOPMENT 6. Recognize how personal attitudes, values, and prejudices affect pastoral ministry (H, P). b. Demonstrate the ability to identify and manage personal biases that may limit pastoral effectiveness.	Comments: 0 1 ② 3 *Social Media - 3x a week on Facebook and Instagram: It still bothers me that online outreach is not as effective as face to face. But it still has value, and I must continue to make the effort.*
MINISTRY ENGAGEMENT 8. Recognize the developmental value of actively engaging in community dynamics. b. Demonstrate the ability to recognize and engage in learning opportunities prompted by interpersonal tensions within a small community or group setting.	Comments: 0 1 2 ③ *RCIA, marriage preparation classes, or/and baptismal preparation classes. In the interactions with Hispanic and Filipino couples. I seem hesitant in engaging with them. I need to learn more about their cultures so I can feel more comfortable. This is a new experience for me.*
Judgment & Decision-making 20. Recognize situations where the ministry of presence is the most valuable pastoral response (H, S, P). a. Demonstrate initiative in finding opportunities to be available to others and respond with pastoral presence.	Comments: 0 ① 2 3 *Ministry of Presence — presence before, during, and after Sunday Masses, Attending Parish Functions. Although I'm making myself available before and after mass, it feels to me more like moments of social encounters. How can I make this more a ministry activity than just a social activity?*
PASTORAL AWARENESS 32. Recognize and value the contribution of women to church leadership and parish life (H, I, P). c. Demonstrate the ability to foster the contributions and gifts of women in parish life.	Comments: 0 ① 2 3 *Adult Faith Formation, Adult Spiritual Enrichment. Most of my encounters with women in formation are intellectual in nature. It would help if I could navigate in another ministry that would provide me with other aspects of women's life. Maybe I need to select another ministry for this objective and goal.*

Figure 3. Sample Learner Evaluation

Supplemental comments / observations:

My pastor is very supportive and understanding. He supported my idea of starting a Bible Class, protects my time, and helps me define and maintain proper boundaries. E is really busy, but I appreciate that we share meals together when I visit the parish. Sometimes we are not able to have a full hour of conversation, but that's OK. I really look up at him as an example of a spiritual father.

The Vocation Board was very supportive and offered a lot of insights.

Figure 3. Continued.

Table 7. Sample of appropriate mentoring promptings

"It seems you are more appealing when your spontaneous prayer in the Prayer Group flowed from your heart. Did you see the same?

"Your openness when meeting parishioners after Mass is right on target. It's very engaging. Yet remember it's not just a social activity. It's also an opportunity to highlight sacraments (marriage, babies).

"Its fine to wait to be approached after Mass, but it's even better if you take the initiative to engage someone when you intuit a need. An usher was distracted after the 9:30am Mass and unintentionally ignored an African-American parishioner looking for a Welcoming Packet…"

"During your visits to families in the parish, feel free to ask about their prayer life as a Domestic Church…"

"You were asked questions about gay marriage in one of your presentations last month. Don't hesitate to be sensitive but also to encourage dialogue with other members of the clergy."

"Parish closings present difficult situations. One lady was hurt because her entire spiritual life was at one of the parishes that "closed". In conversing with her, do you think she was sufficiently comforted after you spoke with her? In hindsight, would you do anything different?

"The Men's Group had asked you to prepare a reflection for Lent. How did you pick your topic? What was your thought process in selecting the topic of online pornography?"

"We saw that during the parish picnic you spent a lot of time with the Bracero family. Of course, its fine because they could really benefit from your presence, but it's also good to "work the room" (so to speak).

"During food distribution at the pantry you were behind the counter helping fill and give out bags of food. Would it be more beneficial to go outside and meet the people while they are waiting in line?"

"The Vietnamese asked if you could help with their quarterly Mass, but we heard that you declined. What was your rationale?

"We heard there was a heated discussion on women and the priesthood at the Knights of Columbus meeting a few weeks ago. What can you tell us about that discussion? What would have been your approach?

"The altar server training session you gave last month was very well accepted by the boys and girls attending.

"We have a chance to see you lead the Stations of the Cross on Lenten Fridays. If Father Bill (Pastor) agrees, would you be OK in offering a brief reflection at the beginning? What topics would you consider?"

"You assisted Father Dan with the funeral of baby-newborn Michaela Hennesey. Can you share with us some of your impressions?"

Table 8. Facilitator Roles

Facilitator Roles:
- Assigned and trained by the Program Director.
- Ensures fulfillment of Teaching Parish polices and procedures.
- Serves as a resource for mentoring board activities.
- Provides skills training on pastoral mentoring.
- Provides assessments of board mentoring performance.
- Provides information on mentoring board formation and resource needs.
- Contributes to designing and implementing Teaching Parish initiatives.

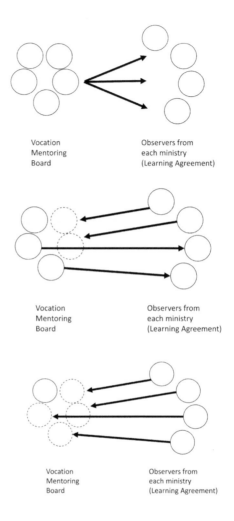

Figure 3, Possible Models for the Vocation Mentoring Board

These are then reported back to the board. A second model is where only the president (or leader) of the board is permanent, and the members vary according to the learner's assigned ministries. This means the board members may vary depending on the agreed-upon selection of ministries. A third model is a hybrid, where some members are permanent, and representatives from ministries are included on an "as needed" basis. What matters to the board is establishing the optimal model given its way of collecting experiences, its internal mentoring abilities, the contents of the learning plan, and the parish's capabilities as a teaching parish.

C. Program Evaluation-Parish Teaching Program

Assessing the pastoral program's effectiveness and areas of improvement can occur either internally or by an external agency. Internally, the program director or the dean of pastoral formation can have evaluation forms for the learners and for the parishes. Vocation Mentoring Board assessments can be reported back by means of the facilitators, the learner, or the pastor. A less common approach is an external evaluation, which is typically conducted using criteria from Church guidelines.

Yet most important to the program is the effectiveness perceived by the learners. A suggested form for assessing learner perceptions is presented in Figure 4. The form intends to evaluate seven key areas of a program, namely, pastoral experiences, experiences with the pastor, experiences with the Vocation Mentoring Board (or committee, group), the ministry environment, achievement of pastoral objectives, and overall program effectiveness.

Figure 4, Sample Learner Assessment

Please check your responses to each of the statements below:

1. The Vocation Mentoring Board was able to provide me with constructive feedback.
    O Strongly Agree
    O Agree
    O Not sure.
    O Disagree
    O Strongly Disagree

2. I was able to meet or exceed my pastoral learning objectives.
    O Strongly Agree
    O Agree
    O Not sure.
    O Disagree
    O Strongly Disagree

3. The pastor was able to provide more useful observations than the parish committee.
    O Strongly Agree
    O Agree
    O Not sure.
    O Disagree
    O Strongly Disagree

4. The teaching parish program added value to my personal development.
    O Strongly Agree
    O Agree
    O Not sure.
    O Disagree
    O Strongly Disagree

5. The pastor was supportive of my pastoral learning needs.
   - O Strongly Agree
   - O Agree
   - O Not sure.
   - O Disagree
   - O Strongly Disagree

6. I consider myself fully engaged in the parish learning process.
   - O Strongly Agree
   - O Agree
   - O Not sure.
   - O Disagree
   - O Strongly Disagree

7. The experiences in the parish helped me make discoveries about my vocation.
   - O Strongly Agree
   - O Agree
   - O Not sure.
   - O Disagree
   - O Strongly Disagree

8. The participants in the assigned ministry were active in my pastoral learning process.
   - O Strongly Agree
   - O Agree
   - O Not sure.
   - O Disagree
   - O Strongly Disagree

9. I had the opportunity to reflect and process the relevance of the pastoral experiences to my personal development.
   - O Strongly Agree
   - O Agree
   - O Not sure.
   - O Disagree
   - O Strongly Disagree

10. The Teaching Parish Committee was beneficial in helping me reflect and process my pastoral experiences.
- O Strongly Agree
- O Agree
- O Not sure.
- O Disagree
- O Strongly Disagree

11. The ministry leadership understood the purpose of my presence among them.
- O Strongly Agree
- O Agree
- O Not sure.
- O Disagree
- O Strongly Disagree

12. The teaching parish program has been an effective way to develop a wider understanding of parish life.
- O Strongly Agree
- O Agree
- O Not sure.
- O Disagree
- O Strongly Disagree

13. The pastoral objectives for this past semester at the parish were clearly defined.
- O Strongly Agree
- O Agree
- O Not sure.
- O Disagree
- O Strongly Disagree

14. I think the Parish Teaching Program provided me with a worthwhile pastoral experience.

    O Strongly Agree

    O Agree

    O Not sure.

    O Disagree

    O Strongly Disagree

15. If I had to give a grade the Parish Teaching Program, I'd give it a:

(Circle your choice)

90-100	A	Excellent
80-89	B	Good
75-79	C	Satisfactory
70-74	D	Passing
69 & Below	F	Not Passing
	I	Incomplete
	NG	No Grade

Thank you for the responses. Please forward your response sheet to the activity facilitator.

Two statements were designed for each of these seven areas and were placed in an order established by a random number generator. The entire Test Specification Table and scoring card for this form is shown in Table 9.

Table 9. Test Specification Table and Scoring Card

Seven Areas of Assessment	Test Specification Table Statements for data collection survey
Pastoral experiences SCORE_____	14. I think the Parish Teaching Program provided me with a worthwhile pastoral experience. 7. The experiences in the parish helped me make discoveries about my vocation.
Pastor SCORE_____	5. The pastor was supportive of my pastoral learning needs. 3. The pastor was able to provide more useful observations than the parish committee.
Seminarian SCORE_____	9. I had the opportunity to reflect and process the relevance of the pastoral experiences to my personal development. 6. I consider myself fully engaged in the parish learning process.
Parish Committee SCORE_____	10. The Teaching Parish Committee was beneficial in helping me reflect and process my pastoral experiences. 1. The Teaching Parish Committee was able to provide me with constructive feedback.
Ministry Environment SCORE_____	8. The participants in the assigned ministry were active in my pastoral learning process. 11. The ministry leadership understood the purpose of my presence among them.
Pastoral Objectives SCORE_____	13. The pastoral objectives for this past semester at the parish were clearly defined. 2. I was able to meet or exceed my pastoral learning objectives.
Program Effectiveness SCORE_____	4. The teaching parish program added value to my personal development. 12. The teaching parish program has been an effective way to develop a wider understanding of parish life.

BIBLIOGRAPHY

Anderson, Marc H., and Peter YT Sun. "Reviewing leadership styles: Overlaps and the need for a new 'full range' theory." *International Journal of Management Reviews* 19, no. 1(2017): 76-96.

Association of Pastoral Ministers, *Competency-Based Standards for Pastoral Ministry*. Archdiocese of St Paul and Minneapolis (ND).

Barlow, Cassie B., Mark Jordan, and William H. Hendrix. "Character assessment: An examination of leadership levels." *Journal of Business and Psychology* 17, no. 4 (2003): 563-584.

Beer, Michael, Magnus Finnström, and Derek Schrader. "Why leadership training fails—and what to do about it." *Harvard Business Review* 94, no. 10 (2016): 50-57.

Bollich, Kathryn L., Paul M. Johannet, and Simine Vazire. "In search of our true selves: Feedback as a path to self-knowledge." Frontiers in psychology 2 (2011): 312.

Carlson, Erika N. "Overcoming the barriers to self-knowledge: Mindfulness as a path to seeing yourself as you really are." Perspectives on Psychological Science 8, no. 2 (2013): 173-186.

Comstock, Dana L., Tonya R. Hammer, Julie Strentzsch, Kristi Cannon, Jacqueline Parsons, and Gustavo Salazar II. "Relational-cultural theory: A framework for bridging relational, multicultural, and social justice competencies." *Journal of Counseling & Development* 86, no. 3 (2008): 279-287.

Conger, Jay, and George P. Hollenbeck. "What is the character of research on leadership character?" *Consulting Psychology Journal: Practice and Research* 62, no. 4 (2010): 311-316. doi: 10.1037/a0022358

Delbecq Andre'L, Elizabeth Liebert, John Mostyn, Paul C. Nutt, and Gordan Walter. 2013. "Discernment and strategic decision-making: Reflections for a spirituality of organizational leadership." In *Spiritual Intelligence at Work: Meaning, Metaphor, and Morals (Research in Ethical Issues in Organizations, Volume 5. Emerald Group Publishing Limited* (2003): 139-174.

Denison, Daniel R., Lindsey M. Kotrba, and Nathalie Castano. "A cross-cultural perspective on leadership assessment: Comparing 360-degree feedback results from around the world." Advances in Global Leadership 7 (2012): 205-228. doi:10.1108/S15351203(2012)0000007013

De Vries, Reinout E., Angelique Bakker-Pieper, and Wyneke Oostenveld. "Leadership= communication? The relations of leaders' communication styles with leadership styles, knowledge sharing and leadership outcomes." *Journal of Business and Psychology* 25, no. 3 (2010): 367-380. doi: 10.1007/s10869-009-9140-2

Dobbins, Gregory H., and Jeanne M. Russell. "Self-serving biases in leadership: A laboratory experiment." *Journal of Management* 12, no. 4 (1986): 475-483.

Duck, Julie M., and Kelly S. Fielding. "Leaders and subgroups: One of us or one of them?" *Group Processes & Intergroup Relations* 2, no. 3 (1999): 203-230.

Ecklund, Elaine Howard. "Organizational culture and women's leadership: A study of six Catholic parishes." *Sociology of Religion* 67, no. 1 (2006): 81-98.

Fry, Louis W. "Toward a theory of spiritual leadership." *The Leadership Quarterly* 14, no. 6 (2003): 693-727.

Fuller, Michael, and Kenneth Fleming. "Bridging a Gap: A Curriculum Uniting Competencies and Theological Disciplines." Journal of Adult Theological Education 2, no. 2 (2005): 163-178.

Gallrein, Anne-Marie B., Nele M. Weßels, Erika N. Carlson, and Daniel Leising. "I still cannot see it—A replication of blind spots in self-perception." Journal of Research in Personality 60 (2016): 1-7.

George, Bill, and Andrew McLean. "Why leaders lose their way." *Strategy & Leadership* 36, no. 3 (2007): 4-11. doi: 10.1108/10878570710745776

Gordon, Angela, and Gary Yukl. "The future of leadership research: Challenges and opportunities." *German Journal of Human Resource Management* 18, no. 3 (2004): 359-365.

Harms, Peter D., Seth M. Spain, and Sean T. Hannah. "Leader development and the dark side of personality." *The Leadership Quarterly* 22, no. 3 (2011): 495-509.

Helsel, P. B. "A Life with Roots: Narrative Pastoral Care and Communities of Identity in the Parable of the "Good Soil"." Pastoral Psychology 61, no. 4 (2012): 485-498.

Hertneky, Robbie Palmer. "The Role of Balance in Women's Leadership Self-Identity." Advancing Women in Leadership 30, no. 14 (2010). doi: 10.18738/awl.v30i0.298

Houghton, Jeffery D., Christopher P. Neck, and Sukumarakurup Krishnakumar. "The what, why, and how of spirituality in the workplace revisited: A 14-year update and extension." Journal of Management, Spirituality & Religion 13, no. 3 (2016): 177-205.

Jankowski, Katherine, Lauren C. Vanderwerker, Kathryn M. Murphy, Martin Montonye, and A. Meigs Ross. "Change in pastoral skills, emotional intelligence, self-reflection, and social desire. Demonstrate the ability across a unit of CPE." Journal of Health Care Chaplaincy 15, no. 2 (2008): 132-148.

Johnston, Payson. "Business and Organizational Leadership as a Vocation: A Renewed Approach to Business." University of San Francisco (2005).

Kotterman, James. "Leadership versus management: What's the difference?." The Journal for Quality and Participation 29, no. 2 (2006): 13-17.

Karadag, Engin. "Spiritual Leadership and Organizational Culture: A Study of Structural Equation Modeling." Educational Sciences: Theory and Practice 9, no. 3 (2009): 1391-1405.

Kellerman, Barbara. "What every leader needs to know about followers." Harvard Business Review 85, no. 12 (2007): 84-91.

Kuhne, G. W. and J.F. Donaldson. "Balancing ministry and management: An exploratory study of pastoral work activities." Review of Religious Research 37 (1995): 147-163.

Lischer, Richard. "The called life: an essay on the pastoral vocation." Interpretation 59, no. 2 (2005): 166-175.

Liu, D. (2002). Metaphor, culture, and worldview: The case of American English and the Chinese language. University Press of America.

Luft, Joseph, and H. Ingham. "The Johari Window: a graphic model of awareness in interpersonal relations." Human relations training news 5, no. 9 (1961): 6-7.

McKenna, Robert B. and Katrina Eckard. "Evaluating Pastoral Effectiveness: To measure or not to measure." *Pastoral Psychology* 58 (2009): 303-313.

McKenna, Robert B., Paul R. Yost, and Tanya N. Boyd. "Leadership development and clergy: Understanding the events and lessons that shape pastoral leaders." *Journal of Psychology and Theology* 35, no. 3 (2007): 179-189. doi: 10.1177/009164710703500301

Miner, John B. *Organizational Behavior: Essential theories of motivation and leadership. one.* Vol. 1. ME Sharpe, 2005.

Morey, Melanie M., and John J. Piderit. "Catholic higher education: A culture in crisis." Oxford University Press, 2006.

Moutousi, Olga, and Daniel May. "How change-related unethical leadership triggers follower resistance to change: A theoretical account and conceptual model." *Journal of Change Management* 18, no. 2 (2018): 142-161.

Mukwavi, Bernard. "Dynamics of leadership in a multicultural church." (2004): 0970-0970.

Nauta, Reinard. "Task performance and attributional biases in the ministry." Journal for the Scientific Study of Religion (1988): 609-620.

Nauta, Reinard. "The performance of authenticity: Ordination and profession in pastoral care." Pastoral Psychology 51, no. 5 (2003): 425-431.

Ouimet, Gérard. "Dynamics of narcissistic leadership in organizations." *Journal of Managerial Psychology* 25 (2010): 713-726. doi: 10.1108/02683941011075265.

Pernick, Robert. "Creating a leadership development program: Nine essential tasks." *Public Personnel Management* 30, no. 4 (2001): 429-444.

Popper, Micha, and Ofra Mayseless. "The building blocks of leader development." *Leadership & Organization Development Journal* 28, no. 7 (2007): 664-684. doi: 10.1108/01437730710823905

Phipps, Kelly A. "Spirituality and strategic leadership: The influence of spiritual beliefs on strategic decision making." *Journal of Business Ethics* 106, no. 2 (2012): 177-189. https://www.jstor.org/stable/41426665

Ragins, B. R. (2012). Mentoring. In K. S. Cameron & G. M. Spreitzer (Eds.), Oxford library of psychology. The Oxford handbook of positive organizational scholarship (p. 519–536). Oxford University Press.

Rojas, Ronald R. "Interpersonal dynamics in business disciplines: Formulating a hierarchy of relational motives." *Interpersona: An International Journal on Personal Relationships* 9, no. 1 (2015): 114-126. doi: 10.5964/ijpr.v9i1.185

Rojas, Ronald R. "Diversity and workplace spirituality." In Diversity and Inclusion in the Global Workplace, pp. 81-107. Palgrave Macmillan, Cham, 2018.

Srivastava, S. (2012). Other people as a source of self-knowledge. In S. Vazire & T. D. Wilson (Eds.), Handbook of self-knowledge (pp. 90–104). New York: Guilford.

Srivastava, B. N., and P. K. Sett. "Managerial attribution and response: an empirical test of an attributional leadership model in India." *The Journal of social psychology* 138, no. 5 (1998): 591-597. doi: 10.1080/00224549809600414

Speechley, Chris. "The changing nature of leadership." *Measuring Business Excellence* 9, no. 1 (2005):46-52. doi: 10.1108/13683040510588837

Sarros, James C., and Brian K. Cooper. "Building character: A leadership essential." *Journal of Business and Psychology* 21, no. 1 (2006): 1-22.

Schettler. Joel. "Leadership IN Corporate America". *Training* 39, no. 9: 66-77.

Skogstad, Anders, Ståle Einarsen, Torbjørn Torsheim, Merethe Schanke Aasland, and Hilde Hetland. "The destructiveness of laissez-faire leadership behavior." *Journal of Occupational Health Psychology* 12, no. 1 (2007): 80-92. doi: 10.1037/1076-8998.12.1.80

Solansky, Stephanie T. "The evaluation of two key leadership development program components: Leadership skills assessment and leadership mentoring." *The Leadership Quarterly* 21, no. 4 (2010): 675-681. doi: 10.1016/j.leaqua.2010.06.009

Tan, Jason Richard. "Matrices for Understanding Pastoral Leadership and Implications for the Global Landscape of Theological Education." *InSights Journal for Global Theological Education* (2019): 33.

Toor, Shamas-ur-Rehman. "Differentiating leadership from management: An empirical investigation of leaders and managers." Leadership and Management in Engineering 11, no. 4 (2011): 310-320.

Uhl-Bien, Mary. "Relational leadership theory: Exploring the social processes of leadership and organizing." In *leadership, gender, and organization*, pp. 75-108. Springer, Dordrecht, 2011.

Valk, John, Stephan Belding, Alicia Crumpton, Nathan Harter, and Jonathan Reams. "Worldviews and leadership: Thinking and acting the bigger pictures." *Journal of Leadership Studies* 5, no. 2 (2011): 54-63.

Van Knippenberg, Daan, Barbara Van Knippenberg, David De Cremer, and Michael A. Hogg. "Leadership, self, and identity: A review and research agenda." *The Leadership Quarterly* 15, no. 6 (2004): 825-856.

Van Knippenberg, Barbara, Daan Van Knippenberg, David De Cremer, and Michael A. Hogg. "Research in leadership, self, and identity: A sample of the present and a glimpse of the future." *The Leadership Quarterly* 16, no. 4 (2005): 495-499.

Walker, S. E. (2003). Active learning strategies to promote critical thinking. *Journal of Athletic Training*, 38(3), 263.

Wollschleger, Jason. "Pastoral leadership and congregational vitality." Review of Religious Research 60, no. 4 (2018): 575-585.

Zaccaro, Stephen J. "Trait-based perspectives of leadership." *American psychologist* 62, no. 1 (2007): 6.

Zech, Charles E., Mary L. Gautier, Mark M. Gray, Jonathon L. Wiggins, and Thomas P. Gaunt. *"Catholic parishes of the 21st century"*. Oxford University Press, 2017.

Printed in the United States
by Baker & Taylor Publisher Services